Introduction to Law in the
HONG KONG SAR

Recommended Stockists

Australia and New Zealand
The Law Book Company
Brisbane, Sydney, Melbourne, Perth

Canada and USA
Carswell
Ottawa, Toronto, Calgary, Montreal, Vancouver

Hong Kong
Bloomsbury Books Ltd

India
N.M. Tripathi (Private) Ltd
Bombay

Eastern Law House (Private) Ltd
Calcutta

M.P.P. House
Bangalore

Universal Book Traders
Delhi

Aditya Books
Delhi

Japan
Kinokuniya Co. Ltd
Tokyo

Kokusai Shobo Ltd
Tokyo

Maruzen Co. Ltd
Tokyo

Yushodo Co. Ltd
Tokyo

Pakistan
Pakistan Law House
Karachi, Lahore

Singapore & Malaysia
Thomson Information (S.E. Asia)

South Korea
Information & Culture Korea
Seoul

Thailand
DK Book House Co. Ltd
Bangkok

Nibondh & Company Ltd
Bangkok

Pasit Limited Partnership
Bangkok

Introduction to Law in the

HONG KONG SAR

Ian Dobinson
Associate Professor of Law,
City University of Hong Kong

and

Derek Roebuck
Professor of Comparative Law,
City University of Hong Kong

HONG KONG • LONDON
SWEET & MAXWELL
1996

Published in 1996 by
Sweet & Maxwell Limited of
17/F Lyndhurst Tower, 1 Lyndhurst Terrace
Central, Hong Kong
and
100 Avenue Road, Swiss Cottage,
London NW3, England

Typeset by Graphicraft Typesetters Limited,
Hong Kong

Printed in China

A CIP catalogue record for this book is
available from the British Library

ISBN 0 421 56880 1

This book is dedicated to our wives,
Tania and Susanna

PREFACE

We started to write this book some years ago, when the law was that of Hong Kong as a British colony. As our work brought us closer to the date when Hong Kong reverts to Chinese sovereignty, we decided to forsake the familiar knowledge, which would soon be obsolete, and to attempt the more difficult but more useful task of describing the legal system and certain aspects of legal method as we believed they would be from the beginning of July 1997.

It was our belief that any new text that sought to introduce the law in Hong Kong should be based on what the law and legal system will be from July 1, 1997. In this respect, the book reflects what we believe should be the current approach to teaching any courses that seek to introduce the law in Hong Kong. Given that the Hong Kong Special Administrative Region will come into existence in less than a year after the publication of this text, there seemed little purpose in describing the current legal system and its laws. To understand the new system, however, one needs to be aware of certain aspects of the old, and in this regard, we make numerous comparative observations throughout the text. In many instances, this has involved noting that most processes remain largely the same, especially those relating to how the law is made, how it is found, how it is administered and how it is applied.

We have based this description of the legal system and its legal processes almost entirely on the Basic Law. This does not provide all the necessary details and in some cases we have been able to gain further information from Government sources, and decisions of the Preliminary Working Group and Preparatory Committee.

But writing as we are before July 1, 1997, we have been forced to make a number of assumptions and compromises, as well as stating that in some cases something will be done or will exist when we have reason to doubt whether this will be the case. This is most notable in Chapter 4 where we describe the operations of a Legislative Council. As is well known, it is now virtually certain that there will not be a LegCo from July 1, 1997, but that it will be replaced by a Provisional Legislature. The legislative processes to be adopted by this body have yet to be determined but, as this body will in turn be replaced by an elected LegCo (by the end of 1998 or earlier), there seemed little purpose in describing the role of this temporary body.

Given the time of writing, we have also had to use various examples of cases and legislation which pre-date July 1, 1997. This, however, is not a problem as the Basic Law itself makes provision for the vast majority of case law and legislation to be retained after the changeover.

Our objective in writing this text was simply to introduce the law and the various legal processes that will form the basis of the Hong Kong SAR from July 1, 1997. Controversy surrounds the changeover and there are many different predictions of what may occur. Coverage of these issues, however, was never one of our objectives and, while it might draw criticism from some, we have deliberately avoided any topic which is controversial or contentious.

Finally, we would like to thank our previous colleague, Professor Mark Findlay, and our current colleagues, Veron Hung, Harriet Samuels, Bryan Bachner and Tony Upham for their assistance in the early and most recent stages of this project.

Ian Dobinson and Derek Roebuck
City University of Hong Kong
August 1996

Contents

TABLE OF CASES

TABLE OF LEGISLATION

ONE

INTRODUCTION

On July 1, 1997 the former Hong Kong British Dependent Territory became the Hong Kong Special Administrative Region under the sovereignty of the People's Republic of China. This momentous event in the history of Hong Kong saw the return of the Territory to mainland China after more than 150 years of British rule.

During this period, Hong Kong had adopted laws and a legal system very similar to that of its colonial masters. It is this system that remains largely unchanged in Hong Kong today. This, however, is not surprising as it was guaranteed by the Joint Declaration of 1984 and the Basic Law. The Joint Declaration was the treaty between Britain and China, which set out the terms and conditions for the return of Hong Kong to China on July 1, 1997; while the Basic Law, which was adopted by the National People's Congress of the PRC in 1990, forms the constitutional basis for Hong Kong's government and legal system since the changeover. Both enshrine the underlying principle of "One country, two systems". According to the terms of the Joint Declaration, Hong Kong is to remain a *common law* system for at least 50 years after the changeover. This is in comparison to the mainland system of law, which is classified as a *civil law* system.

Article 18 of the Basic Law states that the laws governing Hong Kong shall be the Basic Law and those laws that have remained in force since the changeover in accordance with Article 8. Article 8 describes these laws as the common law, rules of equity, ordinances, subordinate legislation and customary law that do not contravene the Basic Law.

Already, we have mentioned a number of terms and principles that many of those reading this book will not understand, either at all, or fully. What, for example, is a treaty? What are common law, civil law, rules of equity, ordinances and subordinate legislation? What is the Basic Law? The answers to some of these questions remain largely the same as they were prior to July 1, 1997. There have been significant changes, however, and the purpose of this book is to provide an introduction to the law in the new Special Administrative Region, highlighting the details of these changes and their effect. In this sense, the book is quite traditional in its approach. Most of the readers of this text will be law students beginning their Bachelor of Laws (LL.B.) courses or other students studying law as part of another degree or sub-degree course. For them, even the concept of law itself may not be well understood. For others, the interest may be in the actual changes that have been brought about by the changeover.

The book begins in Chapter 2 by discussing the simple question of what is law. In answering this question, we deal with a number of associated questions such as what are the characteristics that make something law, particularly law that we as members of Hong Kong society must obey? Why do we obey laws in the first place? If you were studying for a Bachelor of Laws degree, these and many other questions would be dealt with in your course on legal theory, but it is not our purpose to do more than introduce you to some of these conceptual issues. As part of this introduction, we look briefly at the relationships between law and justice, law and morality, and law and punishment. All of this deals with the important relationship between law and ideology; one of the most important ideological principles underpinning Hong Kong law is the "rule of law". A lot is said about the "rule of law" and its importance to Hong Kong, but what is it?

This is followed by a look at what law does and how, in a general sense, it does it. Here, for example, we discuss the important role of discretion in our legal system. Next, we discuss how law is classified and the purpose for dividing the law up into separate categories, such as criminal law and civil law. This is followed by a brief outline of some important areas of law, such as contract, tort, property and criminal.

Then in Chapter 3, we outline the sources of Hong Kong law. As mentioned above, the ultimate source of Hong Kong law is the Basic Law and this chapter is largely concerned with an outline of this legislation. Here, we look at the structure of the Basic Law, its sections, articles and annexures.

According to the Basic Law, Hong Kong law will continue to be created in much the same way as it was prior to the changeover. This will involve the making of new laws in the form of ordinances and subordinate legislation. What these are and the processes by which they are made are discussed in Chapter 4. Hong Kong remains a common law system and this means that much of our law is contained in cases—the decisions of the courts. How this operates and how legal principles are developed by the courts are also discussed in Chapter 4.

In Hong Kong, we are governed by thousands of laws in the form of legislation and case law. Hundreds of thousands of words have also been written about them. In addition, Hong Kong has been and will continue to be affected by other countries' laws, in particular China and Britain;

this involves thousands more laws and words written about them. In Chapter 5, you are told that all these can be found in a law library. Chapter 5 goes on to describe how to find the information in the library and, having found it, how to use certain techniques to understand what you have found. Finally, we also provide details of the latest computerised systems developed to find laws as well as what has been written about them.

In Chapter 6, we outline the new judicial system of the SAR, focusing in particular on the introduction of the Court of Final Appeal. Apart from this significant change, the system remains largely the same as that which existed before the changeover. Here, we discuss what is meant by the description of our judicial system as an "adversarial" one and the important role played by the jury in criminal trials. We also discuss the relatively new and expanding area of alternative dispute resolution (ADR).

In deciding cases, the courts are mainly involved in doing two things. These are:

(a) The interpretation and application of legislative (or statutory) provisions
(b) The application of common law principles and rules of equity, such as those which govern contract law and trusts.

The first part of Chapter 7 outlines how courts go about interpreting the words and provisions of the many thousands of laws that are contained in our ordinances, rules, regulations and by-laws. Then, we expand upon the discussion of case law in Chapter 4 by examining the doctrine of precedent.

Many laws govern the actual processes that need to be followed prior to and during a criminal or civil trial. This is a large and complex area of law and, in Chapter 8, we introduce you to the laws which govern the commencement of criminal and civil trials as well as the trial process itself. As part of this, we deal with the importance of the burden that each side in a case has in proving their claims, and the role played by the laws of evidence in determining how the truth of a matter is established.

Finally, in Chapter 9, entitled The Lawyers, we discuss the roles of the many legally qualified individuals who work within the Hong Kong legal system. We look at how someone becomes a lawyer and what this means in terms of professional standards and ethics. We also discuss how the profession itself seeks to maintain these standards. Apart from those who practise the law as barristers and solicitors in a private capacity, we also look at the roles of many lawyers who work for the government. Last, we look at how someone becomes a judge or magistrate and the qualifications that are necessary for such an appointment.

Two

What Law Is About

2.01 — We can begin our discussion of this topic by asking two simple questions:

(a) What is law?
(b) Why do we have law?

While the questions are simple enough, the answers are far more complicated and necessarily involve a consideration of abstract concepts such as justice and morality. To understand truly what the law is and why we have it, it is necessary to explore the ideological side to our law.

What is Law?

2.02 — The first problem in answering this question is that there is no precise or adequate definition of law, nor could there be. Law, in a literal sense, covers a vast range of factors. These include laws of science, such as Newton's laws of gravity, or laws of nature, such as the survival of the fittest. Another word we could use instead of law is "rules", but this does not get us any closer to an answer. There are many rules in our society that would not be categorised as law in a legal sense, such as rules of etiquette and Chinese customary rules. Then there are other rules, such as those laid down by parents or schools. These kinds of rules are getting closer to the notion of law because what distinguishes them is the requirement that you obey these rules and that if you do not then you may be punished in some way or another.

What distinguishes legal laws or rules is their capacity to be enforced by the State. Law, in this sense, operates to regulate the interaction between individuals in a society or between individuals and the society itself in order to enforce certain codes of behaviour. The criminal law, for example, makes it illegal to steal. If an individual steals and is caught then the State has the right to bring that person to trial and—if they are found guilty—to punish them. On the other hand, contract law says that if one party offers to sell goods to another party and the second party accepts that offer there is a legally binding contract between the two parties. If one party was to break the contract by not delivering the goods, the law allows the other to go to court and get a judgment. The order of the court may be that the person who has broken the contract pay compensation (*damages*) to the other party and complete the contract, as well as providing for the enforcement of the order.

In this sense, one answer to the question is that the type of law we are concerned with here is the legal law. For many, however, this answer would be unsatisfactory. Your own personal beliefs, for example, may affect how you feel about the law and whether you believe that something is legal or illegal. This will in turn affect how you perceive the law and the extent to which you view the law as legitimate. The personal use of drugs, for example, is seen by many as part of an individual's right to choose. It may be against the law in a strict sense but people take such drugs because they do not believe that such behaviour should be unlawful. This identifies two important concepts in the debate on what is law: obligation and obedience. In these terms, we tend to obey certain rules because we believe we are obligated to do so. This could also be true for rules that are not necessarily legal but is more so where these rules can be enforced by the State. In this sense, an obligation to obey the law is both expected and demanded by the law itself. In most cases this does not involve any conscious thought processes. We do not usually go through a thought process of determining whether there is first an obligation and then whether we should obey. For most of us and for most laws, we simply obey the law because we are told to do so. We are told, for example, that we should not steal and we accept that rule. Why we should not steal is not explained by the rule.

Part of the answer to the question of what is law is that law refers to those rules that have been written down. Indeed, the introduction of written law marked one of the most significant developments in the history of modern society. By writing the law down, a permanent record of the law was created. In seeking to answer the question of what the law is for a particular topic, a simple response would be what is written down. In this sense one could simply look it up. The most obvious example of this is legislation, those laws which, in Hong Kong, make up our ordinances, rules, regulations and by-laws (see Chapter 4 for a discussion on how these are created). Apart from legislation, the other principal source of our law is case law, the decisions of our courts. The methodology of how law is created through this process is explained in detail in subsequent chapters, but again this law is also characterised by the fact that it is written down in the judgments of judges and magistrates.

The other important aspect of written law, especially legislation, is that it is contained in a form that is said to be freely accessible to the public. In this sense, the law is communicated to us and it is implied, therefore, that we know it. Of course we could never be said to know all the law, or even a fraction of it. Because it is written down and carries the authority of the State, however, we are obliged to obey it.

So far, we have described the law as rather static and permanent. This is not the case: our law is subject to constant change. In practical terms this process will involve the creation of new laws as well as changes (*amendments*) to current laws. In some cases, we may even get rid of (*repeal*) certain laws all together. In addition, judges may change the way in which they interpret and apply the law, the effect being that the law is altered in some way. While the detail of these processes is discussed later, it is important to note that the reason for these changes is most likely that society has changed or is changing. Hong Kong today is much different to what it was 100 years ago, or even 10 years ago, and our law and the processes that create it must be flexible enough to take account of these social changes. As will be discussed later, however, the legislative processes that have been adopted are generally unable to keep pace with social change. This in turn leads to criticism of the law and the legal system.

Law and Morality

2.03 — Apart from reflecting changes of a practical nature, such as a new way of doing things, change in the law also comes about because of a change in values or morality. Much of our law reflects the values that are seen as basic to the survival of our society. Many of these values are shared. For example, most would agree that it is wrong to steal. The right to possess and own property is quite fundamental to many modern societies and its protection a value to be upheld and enforced by the law. The person who steals is, therefore, condemned by society, which empowers the State to bring the thief to trial and thereafter impose punishment. Stealing, along with many other crimes, can be viewed in this way: as morally wrong. Even for a crime such as stealing, however, it is important to note that for some this may not be morally wrong. Persons who are starving and steal to feed themselves and their family may see themselves, or be viewed by others, as being morally justified in stealing. Even when we think about the killing of one human being by another, the determination of whether the conduct is immoral or morally defensible may be blurred. This may be particularly true in the circumstances of abortion, for example, but our law also justifies other situations where one person kills another, *e.g.* war or self-defence.

For many other types of behaviour, however, the very legitimacy of the law is challenged. When considering conduct such as prostitution, personal drug use, homosexual behaviour and pornography, there are many who believe that the law has no place in the regulation of this type of behaviour and that such laws interfere in the private lives and civil liberties of individuals. Those who support the use of the law in these circumstances see the law as having a valid role in protecting and maintaining the moral values of a society, because to do so ensures the future of society itself.

Law and Justice

2.04 — The position that you might take in the above debate may be heavily influenced by your notions of justice. It is clear, for example, that many types of behaviour are seen as immoral but are not necessarily unlawful. The selling of arms by one country to another, acts of environmental pollution, nuclear testing or the destruction of food when many are starving are seen by many as immoral. The fact that they are not unlawful may then be seen as unjust. In fact, the connection between law and justice would appear even closer than that between law and morality.

Many attempts have been made to define justice but not one would be universally acceptable. Nevertheless, all societies promote the theory of justice. It is clear, however, that one society or country's notion of justice may be quite different to that of another. In certain Muslim countries, for example, adultery remains a crime. In Hong Kong, many would find such behaviour morally unacceptable but would view a law that made it a criminal offence too severe and, therefore, unjust.

Criticisms of the operations of the law, for example that the police have acted unfairly, or a convicted offender received a lenient sentence, are based on an individual's perceptions of justice. This affects both the law and its administration. In many cases, protections against injustice have become law, for example, laws limiting the powers of the police. Where laws are perceived to be unjust, and this view is held by the majority, then this may be the impetus that brings about a change to those laws. As long as the law remains, then there will be feelings of injustice. Justice in this regard may be seen as an expression of community feeling or as part of the law itself. In Hong Kong, the most striking example of where justice has become an integral part of the law and the law-making system is embodied in the "rule of law".

The Rule of Law

2.05 — Much has been written and said about the rule of law. For some it may be little more than political rhetoric, while for others it is the embodiment of the principle of justice. Clearly, Hong Kong believes in the rule of law. It is perceived as the underlying basis for all our laws and their administration. The extent to which this is true or justified is not the subject of this book. Rather, the aim here is simply to outline the various principles that go to make it up. What is important, however, is that, as a principle of law, it does have certain legal force. Laws have been attacked in the past on the basis that they contravene the rule of law and this has then been the substance of a legal challenge in the courts to that law's validity.

The overlapping principles that go to make up the rule of law include:

(a) Law must not be arbitrary—everyone should obey the law and the legal obligation imposed by the law should be fixed and apply to all. Accordingly, "law" cannot apply unless it has been created by legitimate process and there has been a breach of that law.

(b) Everyone is equal before the law—no one should be above the law and the law should not be applied differently to different persons. All persons regardless of position, wealth, class, political views, religion, race or sex should be treated equally by the law.

(c) Law must be impartially administered—those who administer the law should do so impartially, without fear or favour. Judges, for example, should be protected from political interference. Government officials in deciding to initiate legal proceedings should do so free from bias. All persons should have equal access to the courts and expect their claims to be heard equally before them.

(d) Law must be capable of guiding behaviour—law should be understandable. It must be published in a comprehensible, consistent and coherent fashion. It must make the obligation understood and, therefore, capable of being obeyed.

(e) Law must be advantageous—there is no use in having law that provides no benefits to the society it is meant to serve. Law should provide a framework for social, political and economic order. It should protect individuals and their property from unlawful interference, protect human rights and promote justice.

Having read these principles, many of you will have criticisms of the operation of the rule of law in Hong Kong. Many may say, for example, that there is no true equality before the law or that the law is not impartially administered. You may well be right but the diversity of views is really a product of the notion of justice itself. Every one of us will have different views on at least one aspect of our law and legal system. No system is perfect, nor could it ever be, and in these circumstances our law often operates on the basis of compromise.

If we are to obey the law, it must be fixed and certain. It must be rational and capable of being understood. The fixing of the law may in some cases, however, conflict with our notions of justice. The processes established to create or make law (see Chapter 4) are slow and in many cases are unable to keep pace with changes in the society. This has led, in part, to a discretionary approach to the application of law.

Law and Discretion

2.06 — One way the law tries to cope with the problem of justice and certainty is through discretion. As a concept, discretion is an essential and all-pervasive element in the legal process. It may involve:

(a) A decision by a person to start legal proceedings against another for a breach of contract, or whether to report a crime against them or one they have witnessed.
(b) Decisions by lawyers as to what advice to give their clients or the legal processes to use in resolving a dispute.
(c) Decisions by the police as to whether or not to arrest, to investigate a crime, to prosecute, or to grant or oppose bail.
(d) Decisions by prosecutors as to the type of crime to be charged.
(e) Decisions by judges as to whether something is "fair" or "reasonable", whether to allow certain evidence to be heard, the punishment to be imposed or the damages to be awarded.

As an essential element of our legal process, however, discretion must also conform to the requirements of justice and the rule of law, but all this is the substance of another much wider debate which is not the purpose of this text.

Why Do We Have Law?

2.07 — Law can be seen to protect and regulate society, thereby ensuring the society's continued existence. Without law there would no society, or at least none we would be familiar with. It provides order and a framework which governs and regulates our daily lives. It affects us every minute of every day, it even controls time itself—for example, law in Hong Kong, like other countries, requires clocks to be set against Greenwich Mean Standard Time. The law affects us before we are a born—for example, laws against abortion—and after we die—for example, laws regulating the distribution of a dead person's property. Every day most of us will enter into or continue to be part of contractual relationships. At all times we owe certain duties to those around us. The reason why we have law is connected to what the law does.

What Does Law Do?

2.08 — Law has two main functions: to prevent as many disputes as it can and to resolve those it cannot stop. It prevents disputes by making it clear what people are allowed or required or forbidden to do. Relying on the law, people can organise their conduct. The law also says what will happen if they are proved to have broken its rules.

Of course law differs from country to country and even sometimes between different communities in the same country. The law does not interfere in all kinds of conflict. It leaves some to the parties themselves to sort out or to live with. In one community the law may deal strictly with behaviour that the law ignores in another community, for example, adultery. Wherever law exists, however, it is likely to have common objectives, such as the prohibition of theft or killing (except for the kinds it approves, *e.g.* in war, or self-defence, or by capital punishment). It will commonly prohibit certain forms of sexual activity, *e.g.* rape. It probably does not make every lie an illegal act. It cannot control a person's wicked thoughts but is often concerned with their motives and intentions at the time they committed an unlawful act. Of course, most of us behave within the law most of the time without thinking about it. Other factors in our upbringing condition us to avoid antisocial behaviour.

There are other jobs that law has to do that have nothing to do with controlling antisocial conduct. The law says how a person's status is changed by marriage, divorce or adoption. The law lays down what happens to a dead person's property and whether a will can be made and what the formalities are. It says what taxes apply to whom and what licences are needed for what activities. Citizens can keep out of trouble all the better by knowing those rules in advance and organising as much as possible of their lives accordingly.

What happens if there is a conflict or dispute? What if two parties to a contract cannot agree about its legal meaning, or two cars collide at a crossroads, or someone kills, steals or defrauds? Then the law has failed to prevent the conflict and its problem-solving machinery must be used. The rules of law are then applied to the conflict which arises between the individuals concerned, *e.g.* the contracting parties or the colliding drivers, or between the community and the individual, the killer, thief or cheat. The preventive function of the law has not worked and its problem-solving function takes over.

When the law is called in to solve a conflict, its primary task is to restore and preserve order. Yet it must also strive to do what is fair between the parties. The community expects the law to produce a just result but, to find out what legal rules apply to the conflict, you have to look at the existing law. You cannot immediately make up new law to suit each new case. If the law was not capable of being known beforehand it could not serve a preventive purpose: we would all live in the dark and no lawyer would know how to advise a client. The law must be fixed and certain, but, as mentioned earlier, there must be a balance between certainty and justice.

The Language of the Law

2.09 — Any discussion of the law would be incomplete without acknowledging the importance of language. The law, particularly the English Common Law, has its own language. Legislation is also written (*drafted*) using a specific style. One of the most daunting aspects of studying the law is its language. Many terms, for example "*tort*" (discussed later in this chapter) have no meaning other than their legal one. Simple English words will have their ordinary meaning but a quite different legal meaning. Take the word "*action*" for example. Its ordinary meaning refers to some form of physical movement, while in law it refers to the legal proceedings that one party may bring against another. This is further complicated by the use of terms in languages other than English, such as "tort" which is French or *mens rea* (the guilty mind) which is Latin.

The first question that comes to mind is why the law has this unique and complex language. Part of the answer lies in the historical development of the common law and how it has been influenced over the centuries by different cultures and languages. This language has then become entrenched, particularly through the process of recording the law in a written form and through the language used by judges in their decisions.

Lawyers are then trained in this language. It becomes one of the "tools of their trade" and the mechanism through which the law is presented, constructed, interpreted and argued. Lawyers and other legal professionals, *e.g.* judges, have a vested interest in maintaining this language. It is what they use every day and how they understand the law and their role in society. Because the law is complex, most people do not understand it and are unable to resolve their legal problems alone. In circumstances where we require legal advice then we must seek the services of a professional who knows and understands the law and how it relates to our problem. This is the lawyer's job.

As mentioned in the Introduction, Hong Kong has retained the common law and, therefore, the language in which it is expressed (mainly English). For Hong Kong, this gives rise to problems of legal language not experienced where English is the native language. Already, all legislation is in both English and Chinese. Legal work is already carried out in both languages and there is also a growing use of Putonghua. It will take time for those operating the legal system of the Special Administrative Region to respond to these language demands but it is clear that they will have a major effect on legal development in Hong Kong in the years to come.

The pressures of language will be just one factor that will shape Hong Kong's legal system, but what is meant by the term legal system?

What is a Legal System?

2.10 — We tend to use the term legal system quite frequently without much thought about what it means. We know we have one, so do China, Britain, Australia and the USA. Every country has a different legal system. These differences are important. The Hong Kong SAR is based on the notion of "One country, two systems", but what makes up Hong Kong's or any other country's legal system?

First, a legal system can be thought of as a collection of laws. In Hong Kong our laws are collected in the form of legislation such as ordinances, rules, regulations and by-laws. They are also contained in the many decisions of our courts and collected in the form of law reports (see Chapter 5 for a discussion of what this means).

Next, it is a system of government in the same sense as our health or education systems. The government establishes processes for making and imposing the law. In this regard, law exists which governs the existence and operations of the system itself. A legal system also includes the institutions and agencies—such as the legislature, the courts and police —that have been established to operate the system. It also includes the people who comprise these institutions, *e.g.* the judges.

Finally, a legal system also comprises the ideologies and legal philosophies that that system has embraced, such as the rule of law.

In the above discussion, we touch on many important aspects of the nature and functions of our law. In some cases the discussion is quite abstract, but this is to be expected because the nature of law in any modern society and the ideologies that underpin it can only be expressed in abstract terms. In the next part of this chapter, we look specifically at our law, starting with the way in which it is classified.

Classifications of Law

2.11 — Law is too big a subject to think about easily all at once. It has too many meanings and too many aspects. To make it easier to discuss, and particularly to teach, it is usual to divide law up into traditional classifications. Not all classifications of law work in the same way. One obvious distinction is between our law and their law: the law of the jurisdiction where we live as opposed to everybody else's. Another familiar classification is into criminal law and every other kind of law, which can be classified as civil law. The various classifications set out below are just some of the ones that have been found useful in making law easier to think about.

It is important to remember that when someone comes to you with a real legal problem the issues will rarely fall neatly into one category of law. In the diagnosis of the problem, before using the law to solve problems or resolve conflicts, all the facts must be identified, sorted and analysed together to discover their relevance. For example a client may allege that a factory has polluted the environment; it is the lawyer's job to collect and examine the facts to see whether the factory has failed in some duty of care, which may incur both civil and criminal liability, whether it has infringed national and international laws, and whether its acts have affected public and private interests.

Classifications are expressed in opposing categories. This is because we can think of our law as all falling in one classification or the other. The main classifications include: national and international; public and private; substantive and procedural; common law and legislation; common law and equity; common law and civil law; and criminal law and civil law.

National and International Law

2.12 — All law can be divided into national law and international law. The national law of a country is sometimes called its municipal law. National law applies within a nation. International law governs the relations between nations. Relations between Japan and China, for example, are governed by international law, made either by treaty between them or by convention or custom accepted by the community of nations. The Joint Declaration between Britain and China, which set out the conditions for the return of Hong Kong to China on July 1, 1997, is an example of international law. This is known as public international law.

There is a body of law called private international law (or sometimes "*conflict of laws*") to determine which national law applies to a dispute and which country's court shall hear it. It is not really international at all but a part of each country's national law. Each country has its own rules to deal with conflicts of laws, though there are international conventions that attempt to introduce uniformity.

Within a single nation there may be more than one jurisdiction. In most countries there is some power-sharing between different levels of government: national, provincial, and local. In Hong Kong, we only differentiate between national and local law (*e.g.* Urban Council regulations). In some countries there are bigger differences and regions with greatly different legal systems. That is most obviously true in federal systems like Australia and the USA. This gives rise to a division between federal and state law. Each state of Australia, for example, has its own jurisdiction with its own criminal law, differing in important ways from the criminal laws of other states and to federal criminal law.

Public and Private Law

2.13 — We have just seen how international law can be either public or private. All law can be put into those categories. The general distinction is that private law deals with the legal relationships, and the conflicts that arise from them, between individuals or groups. Conversely, public law deals with the relationships and conflicts where one of the parties is the State. The distinction is not always easy to make. Governments, for example, enter into contracts with individuals or groups and they are governed by private law. Governments also take an increasing interest in all kinds of activities of their citizens and no part of the law of a modern state is entirely private, if by private we mean that the State leaves it to the parties.

Examples of public law include criminal law, administrative law and constitutional law. Private law includes the laws of contract and tort, property law, family law and company law. This is an important classification that allows us to group many of the most well known areas of law.

Substantive and Procedural Law

2.14 — The terms substantive and procedural law describe yet another division of all law. Substantive law can be seen as the rules that govern the legal relationships between individuals, *e.g.* contract law, or individuals and the State, *e.g.* criminal law. Procedural law refers to the rules that govern the processes by which legal disputes are resolved. It contains the laws of litigation (the bringing of a case to court and operations of the court itself) and evidence. This includes, for example, the rules of court that require an action to be started in a certain way, within a certain time and perhaps in a special form accompanied by a stated fee. Documents have to be served on other parties according to those rules; they must be drafted as the rules direct; replies to them must be in the prescribed form and within the time limits.

Rules of evidence are intended to ensure that the court has the right facts before it, proved in the best and most dependable way. The rules usually require the original documents to be produced, where they are available, and will reject copies. They will insist that oral testimony be kept relevant to the issue between the parties. Usually evidence of an accused person's previous convictions will be given to the court only after the accused has been found guilty. The law considers previous offences relevant to the punishment to be imposed but not in determining whether the accused is guilty of the present crime (see Chapter 8 for more detailed discussion of the rules of evidence).

Common Law and Legislation

2.15 — Legislation is passed by the legislature or made by government authorities under powers delegated to them. In Hong Kong, it includes primary legislation in the form of ordinances; and secondary legislation, such as rules, regulations and bylaws.

The term common law is used here to describe the law found in the cases, that is, the decisions of the courts in resolving the many disputes that come before them. Most of our law is in the form of legislation but a lot is also found in the cases. Case law can be further divided into cases which deal with the application of legal principles, such as those which form the basis of contract and tort law, and the interpretation of the meaning of the legislation. Cases will often involve both functions but the effect of the court's decision is to lay down legal principles for other courts and judges to follow in the future. This function and how it operates to develop the law is further explained in subsequent chapters.

Common Law and Equity

2.16 — The distinction between common law and equity can only be properly explained historically as part of the development of the law in England. It is important to understand the distinction because the Basic Law states the laws of the Hong Kong SAR shall include the common law and rules of equity in force prior to the changeover on July 1, 1997 that do not contravene the Basic Law (this is further explained in Chapter 3).

To begin, we should recognise that for all common law countries such as Hong Kong, most of our main legal principles were first developed by the early courts of England. Many of these principles remain today and are still in the form of case law, while other principles are now in the form of legislation (see the distinction between common law and legislation discussed above). In early English history a vast system of case law was established. The system also developed a procedure for ensuring that the law continued to be applied from future court to future court. This was known as the doctrine of precedent and still forms the basis for case law today (see Chapters 4 and 7 for further discussion). This led, however, to a rigid and uncompromising application of the law by the common law courts and, in response to this, other courts were established to provide for a more flexible approach. These were the courts of equity, the most well known in England being the Court of Chancery. Thus you would select your court depending on which remedy to your dispute you were seeking. Today, there are no separate courts, but lawyers still talk about common law and equitable remedies.

The following example may help you to understand the distinction. Suppose there are two neighbours, Mr Chung and Mr Wang. Mr Chung's property borders a main road, while Mr Wang's property is located behind Mr Chung's. For the past 10 years, Mr Wang has gained access to his land by a path which runs along the side of Mr Chung's land. According to the title of the land, the path is on Mr Chung's land. Mr Chung has recently sold his land to a Mr Leung. After the sale, Mr Leung erected a gate across the path, which blocked Mr Wang's access. Mr Leung also said that Mr Wang must pay every time he uses the path. Under common law, Mr Wang may have no remedy. The land belongs to Mr Leung and that is that. In equity, however, Mr Wang may be able to ask the court to order Mr Leung to allow him access. If you later study property law, you will find out why but the answer lies in the rights that Mr Wang has obtained due to the 10 years of prior, unconditional use.

Common Law and Civil Law

2.17 — All those jurisdictions where the predominant legal tradition has come either directly from England, like most former British colonies such as Hong Kong, or indirectly from one of those former colonies, *e.g.* the USA, share membership in the common law family of legal systems. Those countries whose legal systems are most influenced by the Roman law, that is the law of the former Roman Empire, are called civil law jurisdictions. They include not only most of the major nations of Western Europe, such as France, Germany, Italy, Spain and Portugal (though not Scandinavia), and their former colonies but also many countries that were never colonies but chose (for whatever reason) to follow their example, such as China, Japan and Thailand.

The essence of the distinction lies in the role played by case law. As mentioned above, many of the legal principles of a common law system are contained in the decisions of the courts. These principles are then maintained by the doctrine known as precedent. In civil law systems, the courts' function is more one of simply applying the law which exists in legislative form, such as codes, *e.g.* the Civil and Criminal Laws of the People's Republic of China.

Criminal Law and Civil Law

2.18 — A distinction is sometimes drawn between criminal law and all other kinds of law, then labelled "civil law". These categories are sometimes used in describing the kind of work a lawyer specialises in—civil or criminal—as well as the jurisdiction of the courts (see Chapter 6 for further explanation).

Classifying the law not only helps us to teach and study the law, it assists in finding the law. In dealing with any legal problem half the job is first finding the law; having found it, the other half is knowing how to use and apply it. Finding the law involves various stages of identification and then further defining or narrowing the scope of what you are looking for. We can observe how this works by looking again at the classification of public and private law. On their own they do not assist us to any great extent, but even if you had just a little legal education your ability to identify the law more precisely may be enhanced. Trained lawyers should be able to be more precise but even they will have to research and better define the law involved in any particular problem. Chapter 5 discusses how you go about finding the law and how you might then apply it.

Identifying the Law

2.19 — In the following hypothetical example we can observe how the process of identification might work.

The case concerns a Mr Fernandez. Mr Fernandez is a diplomat attached to the Brazilian Consulate in Hong Kong. He has just purchased a new Mercedes car from the dealer. Unbeknown to Mr Fernandez, the brakes of the car were wrongly fitted by a worker at the Mercedes factory in Germany. While driving his car from his home to his office, his brakes failed and he crashed into a group of pedestrians who were crossing the road. One of the pedestrians, a Mrs Chan, was killed and another two suffered serious injuries. Before the police arrived Mr Fernandez left the scene of the accident in a taxi. As a result, no one present at the accident knew who the driver of the Mercedes was. When he got home Mr Fernandez was very upset and quarrelled with his Hong Kong Chinese wife, Mary. During the course of the argument, he hit Mary, cutting her lip. This was not the first time Mr Fernandez had hit his wife and Mary decided to leave him and take their two children to her mother's house.

Two days later, the police found out that Mr Fernandez was the driver of the car and where he lived. They went immediately to the address but found out that Mr Fernandez had left Hong Kong and returned to Brazil. Mary has now decided that she wants a divorce and custody of the children.

The task here is not to determine the legal responsibility (*liability*) of any of the persons involved, but simply to identify all the law involved. A good way to start is the chronological order in which things occur.

First we are told that Mr Fernandez is a diplomat. In some cases diplomats from other countries are immune from criminal prosecution. This involves international law. Next, Mr Fernandez has bought a new Mercedes from a dealer in Hong Kong. He has a contract with that dealer that will have a number of terms and conditions which relate to the quality of the car he has been sold. Connected to this is the obligation that the manufacturer may have to make sure that a car that leaves the factory is not faulty and liable to cause injuries. In terms of the possible damage done to the car, can Mr Fernandez get compensation for any damage caused to the car? This would involve both contract and tort law.

One person has been killed and two others seriously injured in the accident. The first thing to consider is whether Mr Fernandez has committed any crimes. He has killed someone and on the face of it this may be what is called homicide. He left the scene of the accident and this may also be a criminal offence. What about the family of Mrs Chan and those who suffered personal injuries? No doubt they would want compensation and they would seek this under the principles of tort law. Against whom would they take legal action, Mr Fernandez, the dealer, or the manufacturer?

When Mr Fernandez went home he struck his wife cutting her lip. This would appear to be an assault and, therefore, a crime. As a result, his wife Mary left him and is now seeking a divorce and custody of the children. This would involve family law. Finally, Mr Fernandez has returned to Brazil. A number of issues arise from this. First, how might the Hong Kong Government attempt to get Mr Fernandez to return to Hong Kong to face trial, particularly if he refuses to do so. This would involve a legal process known as extradition and is part of international law. What about Mrs Chan's family and the other persons who were injured? They may be able to seek compensation from the Mercedes dealer in Hong Kong, but what about Mr Fernandez, who is now in Brazil and the Mercedes company, which is located in Germany?

The identification of these broad categories of law and some of the related issues would be just the first step, but an important one. If you were a lawyer representing any of the parties involved or just a student wanting to determine the liability of Mr Fernandez, the dealer and the manufacturer, you would need to look further and to define the law more accurately. One of the first places to look would be in the legislation. Are there any ordinances which cover the situation? Next we would need to explore the case law. Are there any important cases that will give us our answers?

The above example and some of the thought processes involved tell us a lot about our law and the many complex processes that are involved in its application. They are not fully explained here because the purpose is just to illustrate the multitude of legal issues that might comprise any one of thousands of situations like that of Mr Fernandez. The following chapters will hopefully help you to understand a lot more about what has been introduced here. To begin, we can look at the sources of our law, that is where it comes from.

THREE

WHERE LAW COMES FROM

3.01 — This chapter tries to show how answers can be found to the questions: where does law come from; who decides what the law is; how do you tell which law prevails? From July 1, 1997 the first place to look for answers to these questions became the Basic Law (see Appendix I) as this is the principal source of our law in Hong Kong. Before going on to look at the above questions it is appropriate, therefore, to outline briefly the main features of this law.

The Basic Law is the constitution of the Hong Kong Special Administrative Region (SAR), which the governments of the People's Republic of China (PRC) and the United Kingdom (UK) agreed upon in their Joint Declaration of 1984. It is divided into chapters and each chapter into sections called articles. It starts with a general introduction, the Preamble, which explains how it came about. While all of the Basic Law is set out in Appendix I, it is worth restating the Preamble here.

> "Hong Kong has been part of China's territory since ancient times, but it was occupied by Britain after the Opium War in 1840. On 19 December 1984, the Chinese and British Governments signed the Joint Declaration on the Question of Hong Kong, affirming that the Government of the People's Republic of China will resume the exercise of sovereignty over Hong Kong on 1 July 1997, thus fulfilling the long-cherished common aspiration of the entire Chinese people for the recovery of Hong Kong.
>
> In order to uphold national unity and territorial integrity and to maintain Hong Kong's prosperity and stability, and taking account of the history of Hong Kong and its realities, the People's Republic of China has decided that upon China's resumption of the exercise of sovereignty over Hong Kong, a Hong Kong Special Administrative Region will be established in accordance with the provisions of Article 31 of the Constitution of the People's Republic of China and that, under the principle of 'one country, two systems', socialist system and policies will not be practised in Hong Kong. The basic policies of the People's Republic of China regarding Hong Kong

> have been elaborated by our government in the Sino-British Joint Declaration.
>
> In accordance with the Constitution of the People's Republic of China, the National People's Congress hereby enacts the Basic Law of the Hong Kong Special Administrative Region of the People's Republic of China, prescribing the systems to be practised in the Hong Kong Special Administrative Region, in order to ensure the implementation of the basic policies of the People's Republic of China regarding Hong Kong."

The first thing to notice is that the Basic Law is enacted by the National People's Congress of the PRC. It creates a new legal entity, the Hong Kong Special Administrative Region (SAR), which Article 11 describes as "a local administrative region of the PRC, enjoying a high degree of autonomy, . . . directly under the Central People's Government." The Central People's Government retains responsibility for foreign affairs and defence.

Chapter I, General Principles, sets out a number of broad provisions regarding the SAR. These include the requirement that all members of the executive authorities and legislature be permanent Hong Kong residents (Article 3). Article 5 provides for the maintenance of the previous capitalist system in Hong Kong for 50 years after the changeover. Article 8, which will be dealt with later, specifies the laws which were previously in force and will continue to operate in the new SAR. Article 9 provides for both Chinese and English as official languages.

Chapter II sets out the provisions governing the relationship between the Hong Kong SAR government and the Central Government of the PRC. The SAR is designated as a local administrative region. Responsibility for its foreign affairs and defence lie with the Central Government. The head of the Hong Kong government is the Chief Executive who, along with all other principal executive officers, is appointed by the Central Government (Article 15). Article 17 vests the SAR with legislative power but all enactments must be reported to the Standing Committee of the National People's Congress (see Chapter 4 for further details). The sources of Hong Kong law are set out in Article 18 (discussed later). Under Article 19, Hong Kong is given independent judicial power, except for certain restrictions on its jurisdiction (see Chapter 6 for further discussion).

3.02 — Chapter III is an extremely important section. It deals with the rights and duties of Hong Kong residents. It begins by specifying who is eligible to be an SAR permanent resident (Article 24). This is followed by a series of Articles dealing with human rights. These include equality, freedoms of speech, the press, and association and the right to strike. Freedom of conscience and religion are also guaranteed. Under Article 39, it is stipulated that the provisions of the International Covenant on Civil and Political Rights and the International Covenant on Economic, Social and Cultural Rights also apply to the SAR.

The political structure of the SAR is set out in Chapter IV. This part starts with the position of the Chief Executive, outlining the conditions of appointment and powers. In carrying out the duties of office, the Chief Executive is assisted by an Executive Council (Exco). This is followed in Section 2 by details of the executive branch of the Government. Article 60 states that the head of Government is the Chief Executive. Section 3 deals with the legislature, who can be members and how it is to be elected. It goes on to outline its operational structure and the role of the President of the Legislative Council, followed by its powers and functions (Article 73).

Section 4 outlines the provisions relevant to the judicial system, its structure, functions, and powers. These are fully discussed in Chapter 6.

Section 5 provides for local government in the form of district organisations, *i.e.* the District Boards. Section 6 deals with public servants. They must all be permanent residents, except those from other countries who hold permanent Hong Kong identity cards. Only Chinese citizens with no right of abode elsewhere can hold the senior positions of Secretary, Deputy Secretary, Director of Bureaux, Commissioner Against Corruption, Director of Audit, Commissioner of Police, Director of Immigration and Commissioner of Customs and Excise (Article 101).

3.03 — In accordance with the "One country, two systems" philosophy, Chapter V provides for the maintenance of an economic structure for the SAR distinct from that of mainland China. This covers matters such as finance, trade, industry, commerce, leasing of land, shipping and civil aviation. Similarly, Chapter VI sets out provisions for an SAR education system, scientific development programme, cultural and religious freedoms, professional organisations, sports policies and social welfare programmes.

Chapter VII contains the provisions concerning Hong Kong's external affairs. This covers such matters as the application of international agreements and the power of the SAR to issue passports.

Chapter VIII deals with the interpretation and amendment of the Basic Law. Article 158 gives power to the courts of the SAR to interpret the Basic Law but they must do so in accordance with directions from the Standing Committee of the NPC, discussed further in Chapters 6 and 7. Finally, the SAR Government has the power to propose amendments to the Basic Law but they must be agreed to and passed by the

National People's Congress (NPC). Before a proposal for amendment can be put before the NPC it must be agreed to by two-thirds of Legco and by the Chief Executive.

The Basic Law concludes with a number of Annexures. Annex I outlines the procedures for the selection of the Chief Executive. Annex II contains the method for the formation of the Legislative Council and its voting procedures and Annex III, the National Laws of the PRC that apply to the SAR. These include, for example, the Nationality Law of the People's Republic of China.

Sources of Law

3.04 — As mentioned above, the principal source of law in the SAR is the Basic Law. It is this law which provides the constitutional framework for the Region. All law must be in accordance with its provisions, both in terms of new law as well as that which has been carried over after the changeover. This is stated quite clearly in Article 18:

> "The laws of the Hong Kong Special Administrative Region shall be this Law, the laws previously in force in Hong Kong as stipulated in Article 8 of this Law, and the laws enacted by the legislature of the Hong Kong Special Administrative Region."

This shows that the sources of law for Hong Kong are:

- (a) The Basic Law
- (b) Laws stipulated in Article 8
- (c) Laws enacted by the SAR
- (d) Laws enacted by the National People's Congress or its Standing Committee which relate to defence and foreign affairs and otherwise as stated in Article 18.

Because it is the SAR's constitution, the Basic Law has precedence over other laws. New legislation enacted by the SAR will prevail over all other laws, provided that it complies with the Basic Law. Matters relating to foreign affairs, defence and executive acts of the central government of the PRC are excluded from the authority of the SAR Government. Otherwise, the laws stipulated in Article 8 will continue in force. Article 8 states that these include:

> "The laws previously in force in Hong Kong, that is, the common law, rules of equity, ordinances, subordinate legislation and customary

law shall be maintained, except for those that contravene this Law or have been amended by the legislature of the Hong Kong Special Administrative Region."

Laws Enacted by the SAR

3.05 — The new SAR legislature has full power and authority to enact new laws which have priority over all other laws except the Basic Law. The next chapter explains how those laws are enacted. The formal autonomy of the legislature of the SAR is clearly much greater than that of the former Legislative Council (Legco). Without reference to any authority outside the SAR, it may enact any laws it wishes, subject only to the reservations in respect of defence, foreign affairs and the other matters set out in Article 18(3).

In particular, the legislature can change any common law, equity or customary law. Until it does so, however, every existing rule of common law and equity now applicable to Hong Kong survives, unless it conflicts with the Basic Law.

Law Previously in Force

3.06 — Prior to the changeover, the Joint Liaison Group spent many sessions in order to determine those laws or provisions of laws that were in contravention of the Basic Law. In some cases this involved major considerations, such as those concerning the Bill of Rights Ordinance, while in others the process merely involved the removal of references to Britain or the use of the word Royal. Other laws such as the Letters Patent and the Royal Instructions obviously ceased to exist on July 1, 1997. The Preliminary Working Committee's own Legal Sub-Group also made many recommendations, most of which were implemented.

As a result, a number of amendments passed prior to the changeover were not adopted by the SAR Government, and the legislation was returned to its previous form. This includes the Societies (Amendment) Ordinance No. 75 of 1992, Television (Amendment) Ordinance No. 22 of 1993, the Public Order (Amendment) Ordinance No. 77 of 1995 and the New Territories Exemption Ordinance. It is interesting to look at this last piece of legislation. This ordinance, passed in 1995, effectively removed the last remaining example of Chinese customary law in Hong

Kong, that being the rule that only male relatives could inherit certain property in the New Territories. The abandonment of this ordinance saw the return of this customary law.

Case law relevant to the above legislation and any other decisions concerning other laws which have not been adopted by the SAR also ceased to have any effect on July 1, 1997. The vast majority of case law and legislation survived.

Common Law

3.07 — In line with Article 8, much of the common law (see Chapter 2 for a discussion of this classification of the law) continues to apply in Hong Kong. In addition, most of the cases which interpreted and applied the many ordinances, rules, regulations and bylaws before the changeover remain as authorities quite simply because the legislation remains in force. This is the same for those cases which interpreted and applied the many common law principles relating to contract, tort and criminal law, or dealt with the rules of evidence. In most of these cases, the Hong Kong courts simply followed and confirmed the approach taken by three English courts, the Privy Council, the House of Lords and the Court of Appeal.

The Influence of English Law

3.08 — The courts of the SAR may have to decide quite frequently whether existing legislation and common law survives, and occasionally may have to do so in respect of customary law. The laws in force can be changed or developed only by the legislature and courts of the SAR. The Basic Law states quite clearly that it is the law *previously* in force that is taken into the new SAR. The common law and rules of equity, in particular, will continue to develop in England, but those developments cannot change the law in the new SAR. The SAR legislature and courts are sure to be *influenced* to some degree, however, by developments overseas and in the rest of China.

In colonial times, all courts in Hong Kong followed the formulations of the common law made by authoritative English courts. Theoretically there is a difference between statements which are binding on lower courts and those which are persuasive only (see Chapter 7 for further discussion). In practice, lower courts follow the law as propounded by higher courts. How this doctrine of precedent works is described in Chapters 4 and 7. In Hong Kong all lower courts must follow the law as stated in the Court of First Instance and above. The Court of First Instance must follow the Court of Appeal and above. The Court of Appeal must follow the Court of Final Appeal (see Chapter 6 for a discussion of the Hong Kong Court System).

This following of precedent makes sense. There is not much point in applying the law in a way that you know will be changed on appeal. If you are a judge, and a higher court that hears appeals from you has said previously what the law is, it can be expected to say the same again. It is pointless to go against its authority. If you do, your judgment is most likely to be reversed on appeal. Judges generally prefer to go with higher judicial authority, therefore; though, as Chapter 4 shows, they can be clever when they wish to, distinguishing authorities they do not like.

No court outside Hong Kong can hear appeals from any SAR court. The Court of Final Appeal now has the final power of adjudication for all cases in Hong Kong. No judge need fear a decision will be reversed for applying the law in a way different from an English court. Though for a while there will be many judges who will feel more comfortable if they decide the same way as the law is developing in England, they will not be able to rely on that development as authority. Moreover, any judge who wants to branch out from that English path of development will be able to cite as authority for doing so Article 18 of the Basic Law. "The laws *previously* in force" [emphasis added] would seem to have only one possible meaning—the laws as they stood at July 1, 1997.

Article 84 of the Basic Law expressly provides that the SAR courts "may refer to precedents in other common law jurisdictions." Despite what has been said above, and despite the ending of the English courts' authority, Hong Kong judges are likely to follow some developments in England and, perhaps, developments elsewhere in the common law world. In that sense the common law, as preserved by the Basic Law, will develop as a living source of Hong Kong's law with more discernible Hong Kong characteristics than it had under colonial rule.

English case law, therefore, is likely to remain influential. This may also be true for legislative developments. Many of the ordinances, *e.g.* the Theft Ordinance, that have been retained are copies of equivalent English Acts (1968 and 1978 Theft Acts). Prior to the changeover, some (not all) amendments to English Acts were followed by similar amendments in Hong Kong. Similarly, courts in Hong Kong would inevitably follow the decisions of English courts as to the meaning of these identical provisions. Decisions of the House of Lords were said to be binding on Hong Kong courts.

At this stage, the extent to which amendments to English legislation will be followed by the SAR legislature is unknown. The same can be said about the English cases on the interpretation of such legislation. As mentioned above, many Hong Kong judges may find it easier in the short term to be persuaded by these English decisions. Certainly, it can be expected that Hong Kong lawyers may argue that the courts should follow their English counterparts. In the same sense, the SAR legislature may also continue to take an easy line, as was done in the past, and replicate the provisions of English amendments for those ordinances which have copied English Acts.

Rules of Equity

3.09 — The distinction between common law and equity is briefly outlined in Chapter 2, but it is important to note that the "laws previously in force" include equity as well as common law. In this regard, what has been said about common law and the continued influence of English law also applies to the rules of equity.

Customary Law

3.10 — Article 8 also preserves what it calls "*customary law*". It is unlikely that the Basic Law is intended to expand the scope of customary law and it will presumably remain the same as the "Chinese law and custom" preserved prior to the changeover. This is of little practical importance except as it affects land rights in the New Territories, where there was supposed to be customary law that insisted that all relevant land must pass on the death of the owner to his male relatives to the exclusion of females. It is doubtful, however, that there ever was any such custom but the dropping of the New Territories Exemption Ordinance restored this practice to its previous legal position.

Interpretation of the Basic Law on Sources

3.11 — It is important to note what the Basic Law itself has to say about the interpretation of its provisions on sources of law. The preamble states that "the National People's Congress hereby enacts the Basic Law . . . to ensure the implementation of the basic policies of the People's Republic of China regarding Hong Kong." According to Article 11, these policies "shall be based on the provisions of this law" (the Basic Law). It would appear, therefore, that it is not open to the PRC Government to alter those policies from time to time as it deems appropriate. Moreover, Article 19 begins by stressing that the power of final adjudication is vested in the SAR's courts. It will be interesting to see how the judges in Hong Kong, all trained in the common law system and many brought up as colonial civil servants, will tackle the tasks of creating the new law from the old and new sources which the Basic Law provides.

FOUR

HOW LAW IS CREATED

4.01 — As stated in Chapter 3, it is the Basic Law that provides the ultimate source of all Hong Kong law. According to Article 18 of the Basic Law, it comprises laws previously in force in Hong Kong, which have been retained under the provisions of Article 8 (see discussion in Chapter 3) and those new laws enacted by the the legislature after June 30, 1997. The three principal sources of law are, therefore, the same as they were prior to June 30. These are:

(a) Primary legislation—SAR ordinances and laws of the People's Republic of China relevant to Hong Kong
(b) Secondary, subordinate or delegated legislation—rules, regulations and bylaws
(c) Case law—law arising from the decisions of the Hong Kong Courts

The purpose of this chapter is to examine the processes by which primary and secondary legislation is produced by the Government of the SAR and the development of legal principles through judicial decisions. Such procedures and processes differ little from those that existed before June 30, 1997. Given the publication date of this text, however, it has been necessary to use examples from before June 30 to demonstrate these processes. Because we do not expect the process to change substantially, we believe that this does not present any problems.

Primary Legislation

4.02 — The present Hong Kong Government derives its powers to make law from Hong Kong's status as a Special Administrative Region of the People's Republic of China. The specific provisions of the Basic Law are discussed in Chapter 3, but as mentioned there, it is the Basic Law that provides the basic form and structure of the Hong Kong Government.

Article 48 outlines the powers and functions of the Chief Executive. These include the power:

"(1) To lead the government of the Region;
(2) To be responsible for the implementation of this Law [the Basic Law] and other laws which, in accordance with this Law, apply in the Hong Kong Special Administrative Region;
(3) To sign bills passed by the Legislative Council and to promulgate laws . . ."

The laws referred to above are called ordinances and are found in the volumes of the Laws of Hong Kong. Where to find these laws, their structure and important characteristics will be discussed in Chapter 5.

The Basic Law establishes the legal framework for the legislative process, setting out the powers and duties of the Chief Executive, the Executive Council (Exco) and the Legislative Council (Legco). Apart from certain restrictions that are dealt with later, the Hong Kong Government may (guided by the Basic Law) propose law for whatever purpose it considers appropriate.

Legislation Begins with a Proposal

4.03 — Proposals for legislation arise from a variety of sources. In theory an individual citizen can suggest that a new law be enacted or a current law changed. Individual citizens, however, have limited direct access to the legislative process. One common route for interested parties is to contact local government organisations, such as the District Boards or Heung Yee Kuk to express their concerns and possibly suggest new laws or changes to current laws. Another is through the Legco member who represents their geographical or functional constituencies. It will then be the local government organisation or Legco member who presses the Government for the proposed legislation to be considered. These proposals, together with the Government's own legislative programme (developed by policy branches of Government Departments and the Law Reform Commission), make up the vast majority of legislative initiatives.

Green and White Papers

4.04 — Where the legislation proposed is of particular community importance, there may be public consultation. This is usually achieved through the publication of Green Papers and White Papers. A Green Paper outlines the general direction of the proposed legislation and invites public comment. Its purpose is to stimulate public opinion and provide the Government with feedback regarding the substance of the proposed law. As a result of these comments, the Government may publish a White Paper. This usually provides a more detailed description of the proposal, and may include a draft Bill. The community is thereafter given the opportunity to comment on the specifics of the legislation. Green papers are not always required. The White Paper on a Hong Kong Bill of Rights, for example, was not preceded by a Green Paper. Green and White Papers often also refer to general policy, *e.g.* the Green and White Papers on rehabilitation and equal opportunities published in 1992 and 1995 respectively.

The Passage of a Bill

4.05 — Once a proposal has been accepted by the Government, the Law Drafting Division of the Attorney General's Chambers is requested to produce what is known as a *bill*. In accordance with the Standing Orders of the Legislative Council, this document is a draft of the ordinance to be proposed. It may well be changed before becoming law but even at this early stage it is presented and written in legal form (see Appendix II for an example). This is the same for bills proposing new legislation as well as those seeking to amend or repeal existing ordinances. Bills are not law and do not have binding effect until they have passed through the legislative process. The importance of the drafting process is discussed later.

Bills are divided into two categories; public and private. Public bills are legislative proposals that affect the entire community. An example is the Road Traffic (Amendment) Bill 1995 (see Appendix II), the purpose of which was to change Hong Kong law relating to driving a motor vehicle under the influence of drugs and/or alcohol and to provide a scheme for blood or breath-testing for these purposes. Private bills, on the other hand, are only applicable to the parties named in them. For example, the Airport Authority Bill 1995 provided for the establishment of the Airport Authority for the purposes of operating, developing and maintaining the airport at Chek Lap Kok. There are also special bills, the most notable being the annual Appropriation Bill that represents the Government's budget for the forthcoming year.

Bills May Be Rejected or Disallowed

4.06 — Once drafted, a bill moves on to Exco for its consideration. Under Article 56 of the Basic Law, the Chief Executive presides over

Exco and, in consultation with its members, decides whether or not to introduce a bill to Legco or to make subordinate legislation or dissolve Legco. Where necessary, Exco members vote on whether to introduce a bill to Legco. It is the Chief Executive, however, who has the final say on whether a bill is introduced, but according to Article 56, the Chief Executive must give his reasons on the record for not accepting a majority opinion of Exco. If Exco recommends that the bill not proceed, it may be returned to the relevant policy branch for further consideration or it may simply go no further. An increasingly common practice prior to the changeover, however, was the use of private members' bills. The extent to which this practice will continue is not known, but under Article 74 any Legco member is entitled to put forward a private member's bill. Such bills, however, cannot relate to public expenditure, political structure or government operations. Such bills do not require the Chief Executive's consent unless they relate to government policy. These powers are similar to, but considerably wider than those of the Governor before June 30, 1997. In 1994, the Governor vetoed the Human Rights Commission Bill proposed by Legco member Anna Wu. This Bill sought to establish a permanent Commission to oversee human rights in Hong Kong and to hear any complaints on the breaches of these rights, but as it involved the expenditure of public money, the Governor was able to use his executive powers to block its introduction to Legco. In addition to this power to veto those bills which may impact on government expenditure, the Chief Executive may block bills that are seen as relating to government policy. This could be given a wide interpretation. There are further conditions placed on private members' bills by the voting procedures set out in Annex II of the Basic Law. Whereas government bills need only a simple majority of all Legco members to be passed, private members' bills require simple majorities of both functional constituency members and those directly elected from the geographical constituencies.

There is little restriction on the type of law that can be legislated on, but only those bills that conform to the provisions of the Basic Law may be approved by the Chief Executive. Foreign affairs, however, remain the responsibility of the Central People's Government (Article 13). If there is any doubt as to whether a proposed law contravenes the provisions of the Basic Law then the Chief Executive takes his direction from the Central People's Government. Interestingly, the Basic Law requires certain local laws be made. Under Article 23, the SAR government is required to enact laws relating to treason, secession, sedition, subversion, theft of state secrets, the prohibition of foreign political organisations or bodies from conducting activities in the Region or local bodies forming ties with such organisations or bodies.

The Readings of a Bill

4.07 — Once a bill has been drafted, passed through Exco, and consented to by the Chief Executive, it is then published in the *Government Gazette*. This is to give notice of the bill's existence, its content, and that it is about to be placed before Legco for its consideration. In Legco the main legislative function takes place. Once on Legco's agenda, the bill goes through a series of readings.

At the first reading only the title of the bill is read, in effect putting the members on notice of its existence and general purpose. Depending on the Council's working agenda, the bill is then read a second time. In circumstances where the bill is short and not controversial, the first and second readings may occur during the same session. More commonly, the second reading is longer as the Council debates the merits of the bill. The length of time taken for debate, from minutes to many days, depends on the significance of the bill. In October 1994, the Organised and Serious Crimes Ordinance was promulgated, some two years after it was first tabled in Legco.

The Bills Committee

4.08 — At the end of this initial debate, the second reading is adjourned and the bill put before a Bills Committee for fine tuning. Members are chosen to sit on particular Bills Committees according to their experience and expertise. Members of Legco Standing Committees such as Transport, Health and Security may also be members of Bills Committees or may be involved in an advisory capacity. The permanent or Standing Committees serve a different purpose. They have the responsibility for overseeing the business of Legco in a particular area, *e.g.* transport, and determining Legco policy for this area. It should also be noted that Bills Committtees are not restricted to seeking advice from within Legco. They often seek advice from outside sources, particularly where certain expertise, *e.g.* scientific is required.

Once the bill is returned, together with any amendments recommended by the Bills Committee, the second reading is resumed. At its completion, a vote is taken and members are asked if they agree to the passage of the bill. This question is decided by a majority. If a bill is defeated at this stage it is likely to be returned to its source for reconsideration and possible resubmission, or it may be rejected outright. As most bills relate to government business, it is rare that a bill will be defeated at this stage. In the past, private members' bills have been voted down in such circumstances.

If successful, a bill will then pass to the committee stage. This in many cases is a simple formality as most work has already been done by the Bills Committee. Even so further amendments may be suggested at this stage and the bill may often be considered by a committee of the whole Council that may approve or reject the proposed amendments. If there is a need for more detailed consideration, a bill can be referred to a select committtee at this stage.

A Bill Becomes an Ordinance

4.09 — Following this, the bill is then read for a third time and voted on. In reality, this is also little more than a formality and is done on a show of hands. Even then, however, the bill is not yet law. It must first be consented to by the Chief Executive and published as an ordinance in the *Government Gazette*. On the date of publication (or at some other stated date) the ordinance becomes law and all people in Hong Kong are deemed to have notice of its existence and effect.

This is not the end of the process. Under Article 17, all laws passed by Legco must be reported to the Standing Committee for the record. If the Standing Committee, however, after consultation with the Committee for the Basic Law (a sub-committee of the Standing Committee) considers that the new legislation is not in conformity with the Basic Law, then it may return the law. The Standing Committtee cannot amend the legislation, but the effect is to invalidate the law. Hong Kong courts may also invalidate an ordinance through their powers of interpretation under the Basic Law. This power together with other aspects of the judicial process is discussed in Chapter 6.

Ordinances can generally be divided into three categories: ordinary, consolidating and codifying. A consolidating ordinance brings together, under the title of one ordinance, a number of separate but interconnected ordinances. At the same time, minor corrections and amendments are usually made, the aim being to make the law on a particular subject more efficient and accessible. An example is the Landlord and Tenant (Consolidation) Ordinance (Cap 7). A codifying ordinance is an attempt to combine statute and common law and set out all the law on a specific area. An example is the Bills of Exchange Ordinance (Cap 19).

A Case Study

4.10 — On February 22, 1995, the Road Traffic (Amendment) Bill was read for the first time. The second reading was commenced on the same

Legislative Process

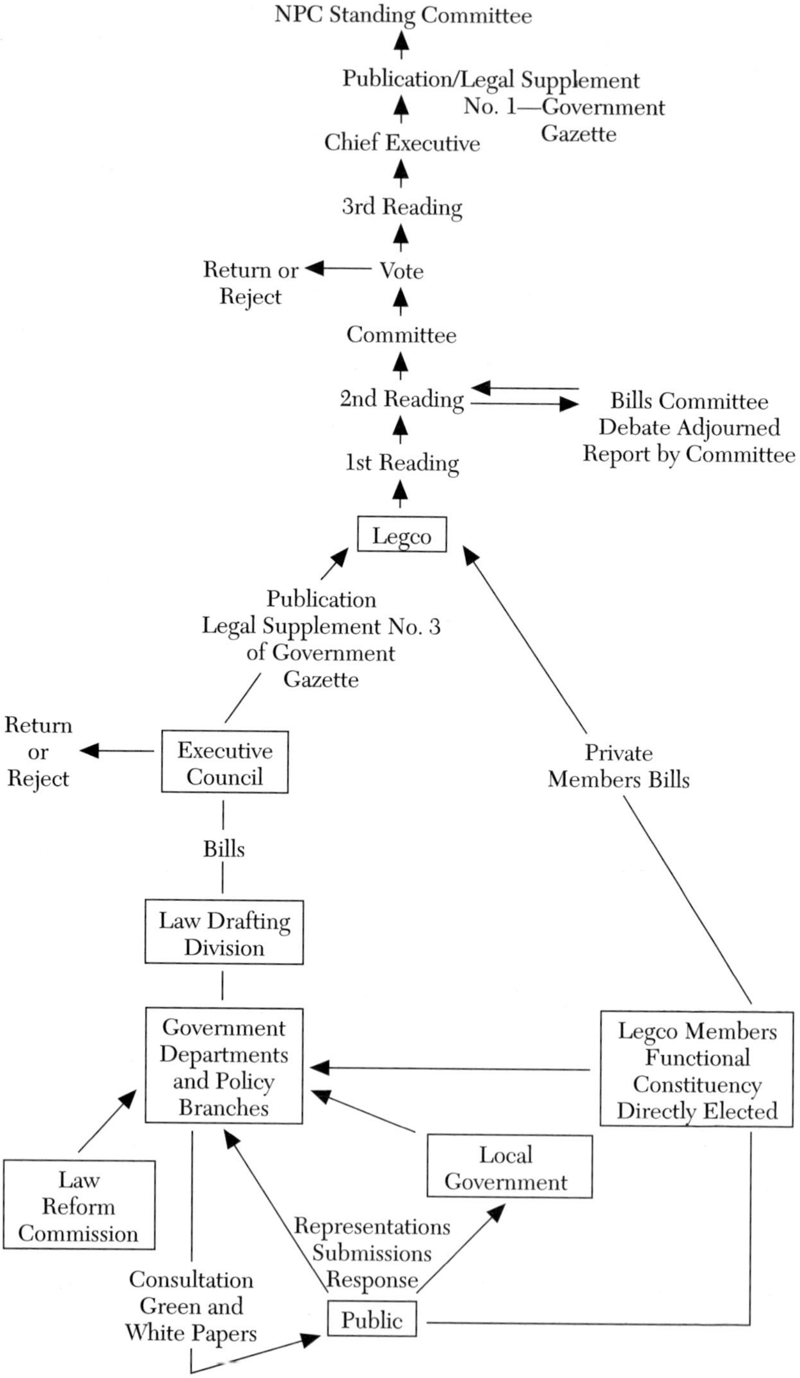

day, with the opening speech by the Secretary for Transport. The main purpose of the bill was to "strengthen legislation aimed at tackling drunken driving" in the territory. At the end of the Secretary's address, the bill was referred to the House Committee and then sent to the Bills Committee. The second reading was resumed on June 7. Mr Wong Wai Yin, the chair-person of the Bills Committee, began the debate by reporting on the work of the Bills Committee and the suggested blood alcohol levels for the new legislation. This was followed by a submission from Dr Leong Che-hung, member for the medical functional constituency. In his submission, Dr Leong called for a tougher approach to be taken and proposed amendments that would lower the prescribed minimum alcohol levels. These proposals were opposed by Legco member Mr Lee Wing Tat, who supported the recommendations of the Bills Committee. Finally, the Secretary for Transport spoke in support of the Bills Committee's recommendations. At the end of this address, the bill was put to a vote, approved and then read for a second time. It was then committed to a committee of the whole Council.

During this stage, Dr Leong moved his amendments. These were then voted on and defeated. The Secretary for Transport then moved a number of amendments that had already been agreed by the Bills Committee. These were put and approved. Dr Leong then moved a further amendment again seeking to reduce the proscribed minimums, which was again defeated. Finally, the bill was read for a third time and passed. On June 8, 1995 it was assented to by the Governor and published in the *Government Gazette*.

Secondary or Subordinate Legislation

4.11 — Secondary legislation is law made by a body empowered by a superior entity to legislate. It is nonetheless law, and is fully enforceable. In Hong Kong, secondary legislation is usually in the form of regulations, rules and bylaws. In all cases there will be a parent law or ordinance empowering the body to make regulations concerning its function. Parent ordinances and regulations are usually enacted at the same time. Some examples are the Urban Council Ordinance (Cap 101) and Urban Council Regulations and Bylaws, and the Mass Transit Railway Corporation Ordinance (Cap 270) and its Regulations and Bylaws. The ordinances empower the Urban Council and the Mass Transit Railway Corporation (MTRC) to act as the supervisory bodies over their delegated legislation, and to make bylaws regarding their operations and functions.

Section 37 (2) of the Urban Council Ordinance states:

"(2) Subject to subsections (1) and (3), the Council may make by-laws for the regulation and control of its finances, including provisions as to the following:
(a) limitations on expenditure by any committee, or sub-committee to whom the Council may delegate powers to authorise expenditure;
(b) the establishment of reserves for particular purposes and the procedure to be adopted by the Council in making transfers thereto and therefrom; and
(c) the establishment of a tender board for the procurement of such goods and services as may be determined by the Council."

Section 25 (1) of the MTRC Ordinance states:

"(1) The Corporation may, under its common seal, make bylaws not inconsistent with this Ordinance or regulations made under section 24 for all or any of the following purposes:
(a) prescribing the terms and conditions relating to the use of its railway services;
(b) controlling and regulating—
(i) the conduct of members of the public using the railway or on railway premises;
(ii) a system for evidencing (whether by issue of tickets or otherwise) the payment of fares on the railway and any contract of carriage of passengers thereon;
(iii) advertising on railway premises;
(iv) the custody and disposal of property found on railway premises;
(c) protecting the property of the Corporation on railway premises."

As with the previous Governor, The Chief Executive has significant powers over secondary legislation regulating public utilities such as television, gas, electricity and water.

Passing Secondary Legislation

4.12 — The legislative process creating secondary legislation is simpler than that for ordinances. New regulations are drafted by the relevant department. Consultation often takes place with relevant parties affected by the legislation before the draft is submitted to Exco. If approved it is then formally placed before Legco. Such regulations will automatically become law after two weeks, unless a motion is moved in Legco to amend them. Section 23 (2) of the Interpretation and General Clauses Ordinance (Cap 1) (see Chapter 6 for a more detailed discussion of Cap 1) allows Legco members to propose amendments within a fortnight of the draft being laid before them. If passed by a majority of the Council, the amendments are incorporated in the regulations, which take effect on the date stated in the *Gazette*.

Case Law

4.13 — Although only the legislature openly makes law, it can be said that law is also created by the decisions of the higher courts through their application and interpretation of common law principles and legislation. Hong Kong cases dealing with common law principles—such as negligence in tort law or the interpretation of the meaning of specific provisions in an ordinance—establish legal principles that will then be followed by future courts dealing with cases of similar fact and law.

The Doctrine of Precedent

4.14 — In this regard, judges are often said to be legally obliged to follow an earlier higher court's ruling as to what the law is when deciding the case before them. The term used is that the court is *bound* by the previous court's decision. In this way legal principles are maintained and preserved over time but, as will be discussed later, this does not mean that the law cannot change. There is considerable scope for legal development through judicial discretion, particularly within the higher courts, to develop and change such legal principles. What is important, as a source of law, is the effect a superior court decision will have on subsequent proceedings between different parties. A binding decision lays down a rule which must be followed by later courts. In common law, this procedure is governed by the *doctrine of precedent*. This doctrine is dependent on a hierarchical structure of the courts whereby lower courts are required to follow the decisions of higher courts. The court structure and judicial system are discussed in Chapter 6, while the doctrine of precedent and how it operates to develop the law is discussed further in Chapter 7.

The binding effect of any decision, however, is not to be confused with the central objective of a court case, which is to resolve the legal dispute between the parties involved, the plaintiff and defendant in a civil case or the prosecution and accused in a criminal matter. In resolving the dispute, however, the judge or magistrate will be guided by legal principles decided in earlier cases. As mentioned above, a court will often say that it is bound by such previous decisions. It is easy for judges to say that they are bound by a previous decision but it is far more difficult to answer the question: What is it in the previous decision that is binding? Where the judge is merely applying an ordinance, the relevant authority is usually obvious, it is the provisions of the ordinance itself. Where, however, as part of the decision the judge says that a section of an ordinance (or a word or phrase in that section) has a particular meaning the matter is more complicated. The judge may be following the meaning given by a judge in a previous decision, or may be giving the words new meaning, especially if it is a new law. Either way, precedent is being developed. In the first case, the judge may be bound by the previous decisions and in the second case the decision may well be binding on future courts. The process, known as *statutory interpretation*, is discussed in detail in Chapter 7.

In other cases, however, the judge will be dealing with principles of common law, *e.g.* the mental element required for murder, or the meaning of "acceptance" in contract law, or the meaning of "duty of care" in a negligence action. Such principles have evolved over considerable time through their application in a series of court decisions. As a British colony, many basic common law principles have been incorporated into Hong Kong law. Up to the introduction of the Application of English Law Ordinance 1966, the reception of English decisions on common law, particularly those of the House of Lords (the highest court in the English judicial system), was virtually automatic, and Hong Kong courts were obliged to follow them. From 1966 to June 30, 1997, however, Hong Kong courts were given more discretion to determine the applicability of English common law and equity to Hong Kong as well as being able to modify it as the circumstances required, though they almost never did. This relationship between the English and Hong Kong legal systems no longer exists, but in accordance with Article 8 of the Basic Law the common law and rules of equity in force at June 30, 1997 that do not conflict with the Basic Law have been maintained. English case law on common law principles followed in Hong Kong, as well as those cases concerning legislation which has been copied here, continue, therefore, to be important. The influence of these decisions is discussed in Chapter 7.

The Development of Case Law

4.15 — There are many classic examples of the case law development of certain legal principles. One of the most famous concerns the duty of care owed by a manufacturer to a consumer which began with the decision of the House of Lords in *Donoghue v. Stevenson* [1932] A.C. 562, H.L. A more recent example concerns the development of the criminal law relating to the state of mind, *mens rea*, require for the crime of murder. Since 1985, the law relating to the required *mens rea* for murder has undergone some important changes in judicial interpretation. In the 1975 case of *Hyam v. DPP* [1975] A.C. 55, H.L., the House of Lords held, in the majority judgment, that you would be guilty of murder if death was a highly probable consequence of your act. This was law in England and Hong Kong until 1985 when the House of Lords (with different judges) decided in *R. v. Moloney* [1985] 1 All E.R. 1025, H.L. that the decision in *Hyam* was not correct. The test was whether the offender intended to kill or cause grievous bodily harm. The court in *Moloney* held that this could be inferred if death was a "natural" consequence of the offender's act in circumstances where death was an indirect consequence of the accused's acts. Only one year later, the same court (again with different judges) further developed its view in *R. v. Hancock and Shankland* [1986] 1 All E.R. 641, H.L., deciding that the term "natural" was inappropriate and possibly misleading. The judgments in *Hancock* suggested it would be appropriate for another court, the Court of Appeal, to develop guidelines which might clarify the position. This occurred in 1986 in *R. v. Nedrick* [1986] 3 All E.R. 1, where the court decided that the *mens rea* necessary for murder was proved if it was the offender's purpose to kill or do grievous bodily harm. If, however, there was no evidence of purpose or desire, then intention to kill could be inferred if death was a "virtually certain" consequence of the offender's act and the offender knew this would be so.

You will deal in detail with this development of case law authority if you study criminal law. The overall effect of these judgments of the English courts is that the law relating to the required mental state for murder in Hong Kong is as decided in *Moloney* and elaborated upon in *Hancock*, and *Nedrick*. This was subsequently confirmed by the Hong Kong Court of Appeal in 1989 in *R. v. Wong Tak-sing* [1989] 2 HKC 94.

Another example of case law development more peculiar to Hong Kong concerns the crime of triad membership. For many years, starting with *R. v. Leung Hon-cho* [1964] HKLR 633, the courts followed the principle "once a triad, always a triad". A person who joined a triad, accordingly remained one for life and evidence of the initial joining was sufficient to prove the offence. In 1985, this approach was altered in *R. v. Sit Yat-keung* [1986] HKLR 434, where O'Connor J. held that this was contrary to the legal principle of being able to withdraw from any criminal conspiracy.

Criminal law textbooks will give you this information on the development of these legal principles, but how would you, as someone studying law, determine how the case law assists you in understanding the necessary elements of, *e.g.* the offence of murder or being a triad member?

Decisions, Verdicts and Judgments

4.16 — Case law in Hong Kong (as in other common law jurisdictions) is found in law reports (for a detailed discussion of Hong Kong's various law reports see Chapter 5) but how would you find the law in these reports? How is it to be identified? At this point it may be useful to refer to some important terminology. A court's *decision* or *verdict* is its ruling on the dispute which is before it. What the court says that a party should do is its *order* or *sentence*. Both the decision and order are part of the written *judgment*. This is sometimes complicated by the fact that in higher courts there may be more than one judge and, therefore, more than one judgment. The majority view then governs the order and the decision, but to understand the case properly you will need to analyse each judgment. As will be discussed later, a majority of judges might agree and decide the case in the same way, but the legal reasoning which led them to that conclusion may be different.

In coming to a decision, a court may have determined it is bound to follow principles stated in the decisions of higher courts. As mentioned above, this is an application of the doctrine of precedent. As in *Moloney*, it may have rejected the reasoning contained in earlier judgments (not binding through precedent) in favour of a later developed or different principle, and may produce a new decision.

When a court follows precedent, or moves on to restrict, expand or reject a legal principle, it makes law. But how can the parts of a judgment which represent "the law" be identified? In most cases, judgments can be divided into a number of common components. These include:

(a) A statement of the facts
(b) A summary of the arguments of the parties
(c) A review of the relevant case law
(d) The judge's determination of existing legal principles, their interpretation, applicability and adequacy

(e) The judge's decisions in relation to the dispute and the effect of the cited case law
(f) The order or decree.

Clearly, the "law" is to be found in the judgment but not all the judgment can be said to be "law". Not all statements of judges bind future courts. Whether someone was killed in his home or in the street could well be of critical importance to a decision in a murder trial, but of little relevance for subsequent cases. This is a decision about the facts of the case and, important as they may be to the determination of the instant case, issues of fact are only important to later cases in determining how similar one is to the other or how those which are dissimilar may be *distinguished*. If the facts are similar, similar legal rules may be expected to be relevant but, as no two sets of facts are identical, any significant difference of a material fact may produce a different result.

Ratio decidendi

4.17 — Similarly, the answer to the question of whether in one case the accused has the required *mens rea* (mental element) has no effect over later cases. What has an effect, and, therefore, can be said to be law, is the test that a court applies in determining this answer. This is the part of the decision that is binding and is known as the *ratio decidendi*, meaning the reason for deciding, often abbreviated to *ratio*. The *ratios* are those parts of a decision which are *central* and *essential* to the court's conclusions. In a criminal case, this is the reason why the accused is found guilty or not guilty; in a civil case it may be the reason why, for example, the defendant is liable to pay damages or not. In appeal cases, discussions concerning the accurate application and the adequacy of a *ratio* comprise much of the substance of the appeal. There can be more than one *ratio* in a case, simply because more than one decision may be central to the ruling, or more than one judge may determine the majority decision. Identifying the *ratio*, therefore, can be a complex and confusing exercise for the beginner. Don't be disheartened, because you will find plenty of examples of judges differing over the nature and meaning of legal principle even in the same case.

In terms of binding precedent, the legal effect of any *ratio* will depend on its interpretation and application by a later court. In this sense, it is a later court that will state and, accordingly, determine what the *ratio* of the earlier decision was. Someone studying law may form an opinion of what they believe the *ratio* of a case to be once a judgment is delivered, but confirmation of that opinion will have to wait until a later case has the opportunity to review the earlier decision and the legal principles on which the decision was based. This would certainly be the case where a future court says it is bound by the *ratio* of the previous case. In such circumstances, we must also note the role played by lawyers (in most cases barristers) who will be arguing that the court should follow a particular decision. What makes the study of law so challenging is that you may disagree with this later court's interpretation, as may judges in subsequent cases. If there is more than one judge in a case, they themselves may disagree. Courageous lawyers have sometimes argued before a higher court for the adoption of the *ratio* in a minority judgment, and the higher court has been persuaded by their argument. What this should tell you is that there are no straightforward rules for determining the *ratio* of a case and that the concept of *ratio* is flexible and subject to the discretion of judges in subsequent cases.

Obiter dicta

4.18 — If judges rely on a legal proposition as the justification for their decisions, that proposition is the *ratio*, at least for them and any lower courts for which their decision is authority. Judges may state other propositions of law which are not part of the *ratio*. Such statements are called *obiter dicta*, which literally means "things said by the way". While such statements of legal principle may not be central to the decision, they are still important. Lawyers will regularly suggest to courts that they should be *persuaded* by the *obiter dicta* of a previous court's decision because they are now central to the matter currently being heard, and because of the authority of the judge or the court from which they emerged. In terms of precedent, lawyers are forced to argue in this fashion because *obiter dicta* have only persuasive force, while the *ratio* is binding. If, however, a judge follows the *obiter dicta* of an earlier case, and they are central to the decision, then they will become the *ratio* of the current case and bind future courts.

How to Analyse Case Law

4.19 — The first step in determining the *ratio* is to identify the *material* facts. Facts are material if they are central to the resolution of the dispute. In the following hypothetical example, Ling is on trial for murder and robbery, said to have occurred at 16.00, Monday, June 8, 1991, in Cheung's jewellery shop in Nathan Road, Mongkok. Ling's presence in the jewellery shop at that time, his possession of the murder weapon and the property that is alleged to have been stolen are material facts. Their establishment will be crucial to determining his guilt or innocence. The fact that he is married to Betty Ling may be immaterial. It could be material, however, if Ling claimed to have been with his wife at the time of the crime. Suppose that the above material facts are proved. It is further established that, during the course of the robbery, Ling pointed a gun at Cheung and, as a result of the gun discharging, Cheung was killed. Ling states in his defence that although he did fire the gun that killed the victim it was an accident, the gun discharging when Cheung threw an object at Ling, striking Ling's hand. Ling says he had no intention of shooting anyone.

As part of the judgment of the Hong Kong Court of Appeal, the court says that it is should follow the decision in the case of *R. v. Wong Tak-sing*. Accordingly, the required mental state (*mens rea*) for murder is:

(a) An intention to kill, or
(b) An intention to do grievous bodily harm.

Further, a jury can infer such an intention where death is a virtually certain consequence of the accused's actions and the accused knew this to be so. The court also says that if someone in the same circumstances fired a gun at the ceiling in order to frighten, and the bullet subsequently ricocheted, killing someone, then this would not be murder because death was not virtually certain. For these reasons the court dismisses Ling's appeal against his conviction for murder.

In the above illustration, the *ratio* would include the statement that the court should follow the decision in *Wong Tak-sing* and what the Court of Appeal said was the required *mens rea* for murder. The court's hypothetical conclusion regarding the ricocheting bullet would be *obiter dicta*. By virtue of the doctrine of precedent, the *ratio* in this case will bind future courts in Hong Kong. The *obiter dicta* cannot bind, but are an important statement of legal principle and may be influential in a future decision.

Majority and Minority Judgments

4.20 — In the Court of Appeal in Hong Kong usually three judges hear the case. Suppose, in the illustration above, that two judges (call them X and Y) dismiss Ling's appeal and one (Z) allows it. By a 2 to 1 majority, Ling's conviction would stand but how does this division of judicial opinion affect the determination of the *ratio* of the case and its subsequent binding effect?

The law created by this decision is to be found in the decisions of the two majority judges. By virtue of the doctrine of precedent, it is only the majority *ratio* that can bind future courts. This presents few problems for future courts if the *ratios* of both judges are the same, but what if they are slightly different? What would be the position if judge X says that death must be "*virtually* certain", while judge Y says that it must be "*very* certain"?

This difference can only be resolved by a decision of a future court. What this highlights is the importance of language, something we will discuss next. What about judge Z's judgment? Suppose he says that death must be "*absolutely* certain", and as this was not so in the case of Ling then for this judge and on this principle the appeal should be allowed. The doctrine of precedent states that his decision can have no binding effect but it still has importance. In a future case a defence lawyer may attempt to *persuade* a court that it is judge Z's test that should be followed and not that of X or Y.

Giving Meaning to the Language of the Law

4.21 — As both case law and legislation are written, the form of the language that they adopt is very important to its subsequent application. Legislation, for example, must be *drafted* in terms that are broad enough to be relevant to whole classes of people, whole classes of behaviour, and broad ranges of situations. Legal drafting is, therefore, an extremely important process in terms of how law is created. As an ex-British colony, Hong Kong has adopted the English approach to this task in terms of the guidelines to be adopted by the law drafter. These include:

(a) Legal effectiveness
(b) Procedural legitimacy
(c) Timeliness
(d) Certainty
(e) Comprehensibility
(f) Acceptibility
(g) Brevity
(h) Debatability
(i) Legal compatability

This gives rise to many problems for the drafter. Not only must the words of an ordinance be general enough to cover all foreseeable instances falling within the policy of the ordinance, but there must be sufficient detail to ensure that the meaning is clear and not misleading. Given the endless possibilities of human behaviour, no legislation could ever cover all possible circumstances. The job of the drafter is to get the balance right between generality and detail, but it will be the courts who will settle disputes as to whether an ordinance applies and what its meaning is for any set of facts. The ways in which the courts go about this task are discussed in Chapter 7.

Case law, on the other hand, emanates from the facts of a particular dispute. The *ratio* that a judge uses to decide the case, especially as it is applied by a later court, may result in it being given a wide or narrow interpretation. This will depend on the language used. Later courts may give a wide interpretation to a previous court's ruling when a narrow one was meant, and vice versa. Judges must, therefore, be careful (like the law drafter) in how they form a *ratio*, and demonstrate their intentions for its future interpretation as clearly as possible.

Wide or Narrow Interpretation

4.22 — The following example illustrates how this often is easier said than done. Suppose there are two neighbours, Mr Chan and Mr Cheung. Mr Chan operates a small metal workshop on his property where he often does welding. On a particular occasion, sparks from his welding fall onto some combustible material stored nearby in Mr Cheung's property. The resulting fire causes $50,000 damage to Mr Cheung's property.

In deciding to award damages to Cheung in the amount of $50,000, the judge states that a person who undertakes welding has a strict duty to prevent the escape from his land of dangerous sparks and that if sparks do escape then he will be liable for the damage which occurs. In the judgment, it is also said that welding is a non-natural use of land and as sparks in these circumstances are equivalent to a fire, a neighbour has a duty to prevent a fire on his property escaping and causing damage to his neighbour's property. One question that arises is whether this *ratio* is applicable to everything on a person's property that is capable of causing damage if it escapes—the wide formula—or only to certain things, *e.g.* those that are not there naturally but are brought onto the land by the owner or occupier—the narrow formula. Alternatively, is it only applicable to cases where a fire spreads from one property to another? What about associated smoke damage or water damage from extinguishing the fire?

Let's look at another hypothetical case. In this situation, Mr Leung is an academic who is researching the media coverage of the last 365 days of Hong Kong under British rule. In his flat he has stored many thousands of pages of local and Chinese newspapers. These subsequently catch fire. The fire brigade quickly put the fire out, but the resulting smoke and water cause considerable damage to the flat of his neighbour, Mr Lee. The cause of the fire is unknown. Is Mr Leung liable in accordance with the decision in Mr Chan's case?

The answer is complex. To begin, you might think that a neighbour will be liable in all cases where there is a non-natural use of property and something on their property damages their neighbour's property. Alternatively, you may consider this to be too wide and conclude that they should only be liable where they have been negligent. If you subsequently study the law of tort, you will learn that there are a number of approaches to this situation and the answer is not easy. Where the meaning is not clear from the language used, or judges in later cases say it is not clear, these judges will attempt to determine what the intentions of the earlier judges were. In this regard, judges exercise a considerable amount of discretion, and through such interpretation can decide whether or not to follow the previous decision.

Distinguishing Cases

4.23 — Judges and lawyers use such an approach to *distinguish* a previous decision from the one currently being heard if they wish to show that the court is not bound. In order to distinguish a case, there must be a significant difference in the material facts or in the reasoning employed. Let's look at the illustration above to demonstrate what this means. To begin, we can distinguish the two cases on the basis of the type of fire. In one case, there are sparks resulting from welding while in the other, the cause of the fire is unknown. In the first case, Mr Chan may also have been obliged to adopt measures to reduce the escape of the sparks. Finally, it was fire that caused the damage in the first case while in the second it was actions taken to extinguish the fire.

It should be remembered that there is no magic formula for determining the *ratio* of a case or whether it has a wide or narrow interpretation. Judges have been given a great deal of discretion to decide each case as they think fit. It is important, however, that the law is consistent and that its application is predictable. Society needs a set of consistent rules and laws on which to base its continued and future existence. Accordingly, a judge's discretion is not unlimited and in Chapter 6 we will discuss the legal principles that "guide" judges in the exercise of their discretion.

Five

Finding The Law

5.01 — Chapter 4 provides some examples of bills, ordinances and cases. If we wanted to find these and read them, where and how would we look? The answer to where is simple: in your law library, but how would you find them? If we know the name of the case or ordinance this may seem an easy task, but what if we are looking for all the law on a particular topic, *e.g.* the *mens rea* for murder or the duty of care owed by one neighbour to another? At a more practical level, how might you find all the law that is relevant to a particular dispute? For example, how would you search for all the law that is relevant to the disputes between Mr Chan and his neighbour and Mr Leung and his neighbour, as decribed at the end of Chapter 4? As stated above, the information necessary to answer these and many other questions of law may be found in your law library. As a subject of study, law is above all else reliant on written resources and is, therefore, library-based. As a law student you can look forward to spending more time in the law library than in the classroom. The initial and essential skills to be gained and practised by any successful student of law relate to accessing library sources efficiently.

Primary and Secondary Sources

5.02 — To begin, we can divide our law sources under two headings: primary and secondary. In Hong Kong, primary sources include:

(a) The Basic Law
(b) Ordinances
(c) Chinese legislation applicable to Hong Kong
(d) Subsidiary legislation, such as regulations, rules, and bylaws
(e) Law reports, for Hong Kong and other common law jurisdictions

Secondary or literary sources include:

(a) Legal encyclopedias
(b) Digests and case citators
(c) Dictionaries
(d) Directories
(e) Textbooks
(f) Legal journals, and abstracts and indexes to legal periodicals
(g) Computerised information systems

Primary Sources

Legislation

Laws of Hong Kong

5.03 — Ordinances and subsidiary legislation can be found in the volumes of the Laws of Hong Kong. Ordinances are listed by name and chapter number, *e.g.* Legal Practitioner's Ordinance (Cap 159). If we know the name of the ordinance, we can find the relevant volume in which the ordinance appears by consulting the index volume. In the relevant volume, the ordinances (referred to as chapters of the laws—Cap) appear in numerical order. If you don't know the name of the Ordinance, try looking for the topic or the issue for which you are seeking the law. Again, the Index may be consulted as a guide to the subject matter in which you are interested. The titles of ordinances often reflect their content and, therefore, the law they create, *e.g.* Dangerous Drugs Ordinance (Cap 134).

At present the Laws of Hong Kong are presented in a loose-leaf format. Subsidiary legislation (regulations, bylaws) is usually found after the ordinance to which it applies, *e.g.* the Mass Transit Railway Corporation Ordinance (Cap 270) and the Mass Transit Railway Corporation Bylaws. New ordinances are simply included in the loose-leaf binders as they become law. Current ordinances and subsidiary legislation are updated or amended by inserting new pages and discarding the old. If there is a substantial amendment then the whole ordinance may be reprinted. The printed Laws of Hong Kong are only as up to date as the last printing of the latest pages. New ordinances and amending pages have to be printed and it may be some time before they actually appear in the volumes of the Laws of Hong Kong.

How then do we find out the most up to date position on an ordinance? There are a number of ways of doing this. First, we should note that the updating of the loose-leaf volumes occurs approximately every six months. Our starting date, therefore, would be June 1997. Each Ordinance begins with a pink page entitled Check List and Instructions. At the bottom of this page is an Enactment History for the Ordinance which gives enactment numbers and dates for all amendments from its initial enactment. The last cited amendment of this history shows the current updated position of the printed legislation. How would you check to see if this was the most up to date position?

The *Government Gazette*, which is published every week (usually on a Friday) contains a continuous record of recent updates to the legislation. The content of these *Gazettes* can be obtained from the various legal supplements to the *Gazette*, which are published in bound volumes: Legal Supplement No. 1 containing new ordinances, Supplement No. 2 Regulations, and Supplement No. 3 Bills. By taking the last number and date in the enactment history, you could then check the cumulative index of the most recent volume of Legal Supplement No. 1 to see if there have been any amendments (Legal Supplement No. 2 if you were checking subsidiary legislation). You could even check to see if there were any proposed new amendments by consulting Legal Supplement No. 3 to see if there were any bills to amend the ordinance with which you are concerned.

By far the easiest and quickest form of updating legislation is through the use of INFO/LAW. This is an on-line full text database of all Hong Kong legislation (including bills) produced by the Government's Legal Department. It is also bilingual. In addition, the database includes judgments of the Hong Kong Supreme Court produced by the Faculty of Law at Hong Kong University. This database allows you to find the most up to date versions of ordinances and subsidiary legislation (regulations and by-laws). Even if you do not know the name of the ordinance a keyword can be used. If you wished you could also trace the complete history of an ordinance. Alternatively, you might wish to find all the legislation that affects a particular topic; you may do this by simply inputting the short topic you are interested in, *e.g.* employee compensation. INFO/LAW will then list all the legislation that contains these words. This is particularly useful when legislative provisions are spread across a number of ordinances and pieces of subsidiary legislation.

You might also wish to analyse or follow the debate in Legco on a new ordinance or a proposed bill. Although such debates do not have the force of law they can be useful as aids to interpretation. The volumes of *Hansard*, the published written record of each Legco session, contain these debates (see for example the case study in Chapter 4). *Hansard* may also be accessed through University of Hong Kong's database known as Law-On-Line.

Once the relevant piece of legislation has been located, you need to

4 **CAP. 32** *Companies*

Section

Annual Return

107. Annual return to be made by company having a share capital
108. Annual return to be made by company not having a share capital
109. General provisions as to annual returns
110. Certificates to be sent by private company with annual return

Meetings and Proceedings

111. Annual general meeting
112. (*Repealed*)
113. Convening of extraordinary general meeting on requisition
114. Length of notice for calling meetings
114A. General provisions as to meetings and votes
114B. Power of court to order meeting
114C. Proxies
114D. Right to demand a poll
114E. Voting on a poll
115. Representation of companies at meetings of other companies and of creditors
115A. Circulation of members' resolutions, etc.
116. Special resolutions
116A. Restriction on alteration of articles to improve director's emoluments
116B. Resolutions signed by all members deemed to have been passed at meeting
116C. Resolutions requiring special notice
117. Registration and copies of certain resolutions and agreements
118. Resolutions passed at adjourned meetings
119. Minutes of proceedings of meetings and directors
119A. Place where minute books to be kept and notice of change of place
120. Inspection of minute books

Accounts and Audit

121. Keeping of books of account
122. Profit and loss account and balance sheet
123. General provisions as to contents and form of accounts
124. Obligation to lay group accounts before holding company
125. Form of group accounts
126. Contents of group accounts
127. Financial year of holding company and subsidiary
128. Statement in holding company's accounts of identities and places of incorporation of subsidiaries, and particulars of share-holdings therein

determine whether it actually contains the law you are searching for. To read every word from the first page to the last would be time consuming and, except in unusual circumstances, unnecessary. Assistance in finding the law within the legislation can be gained from the ordinance itself. For instance, the Companies Ordinance 1984 (Cap 32) Volume 4 contains 367 pages. If you only want to know about the law covering company meetings, you should read the contents pages at the beginning of the ordinance to discover the reference including section numbers (see example on p. 52).

In addition, you may be helped by other features of an ordinance. These include:

(a) The long and short titles, which provide a description of the purposes and objects of an ordinance
(b) The interpretation section (always section 2 of an ordinance), which provides definitions of key words and phrases
(c) Section titles, which contain catchword summaries of the contents of the section
(d) Schedules at the end of the Ordinance, which are designed to elaborate on particular details referred to in the ordinance, *e.g.* the penalties for certain offences

By referring to the Road Traffic (Amendment) Ordinance in Appendix II, we can observe some of these features. Under section 2 the "prescribed limits" of alcohol are specified. Section 7 outlines the new legislative provisions to be added to the Road Traffic Ordinance (Cap 374), being subsections 39A-G. The title of each of these sections provides a brief catchword summary of its contents. Finally, section 14 provides for the amendment of the Road Traffic (Driving-offence Points) Ordinance (Cap 375) by specifying the number of points a driver will lose who commits an offence relating to driving under the influence of drugs and/or alcohol.

Chinese Legislation

5.04 — Article 18 of the Basic Law states that National (PRC) laws "shall not be applied in the Hong Kong Special Administrative Region except for those listed in Annex III to this Law" (the Basic Law). One of the laws listed in Annex III is the Nationality Law of the People's Republic of China. Other Chinese legislation is also obviously important to those studying, researching or practising law in Hong Kong, but how would we find the Nationality Law as well as any other Chinese legislation?

The most up-to-date source of Chinese legislation is contained in the loose-leaf collection Laws and Regulations of the People's Republic of China, which is edited by the Legislative Affairs Commission of the National People's Congress. There are four levels to the collection:

(a) Laws—as passed by the NPC or its Standing Committee
(b) Decisions Regarding Laws—as made by the NPC or its Standing Committee
(c) Administrative Rules and Regulations—as approved by the State Council and promulgated by the various ministries and commissions
(d) Documents with the Effect of Rules and Regulations—as provided by the State Council or reported by the various ministries and commissions

Importantly, this is an authoritative (official) version of Chinese legislation and is updated bimonthly. This collection was begun in 1995 and was initially only in Chinese. Earlier English collections of Chinese legislation include the Statutes and Regulations of the People's Republic of China and the Official Laws and Regulations of the People's Republic of China but these were updated only to 1988 and 1987 respectively. Other English sources include Chinese Laws for Foreign Business (loose-leaf by CCH Australia), China Law and Practice and China Economic News.

Chinese legislation is also available on CD-ROM as well as other on-line services including LEXIS (discussed later) and Hong Kong University's Law-On-Line.

English Legislation

5.05 — English legislation is still important to Hong Kong. Prior to June 30, 1997, a considerable amount of English legislation had been adopted in Hong Kong in the form of a direct copy or modified copy, *e.g.* the Theft Ordinance (Cap 210) and Dangerous Drugs Ordinance (Cap 134). Legislative changes in England to these statutes may, therefore, be important to the study and practice of law in Hong Kong in the future and it is possible that Hong Kong may legislate to follow such amendments.

There are a number of sources of English statutes and methods of finding and researching them. They include:

(a) *Current Law Statutes Annotated*—This is an annual series which sets out the Public General Acts of the United Kingdom. There is also a loose-leaf service for the Acts passed in each year. If you know the date and name of the Act you can simply refer to it in the relevant volume

(b) *Halsbury's Statutes of England*—There are a number of parts to this series. Apart from the statutes themselves, *Halsbury's Statutes* also provides lists of cases relevant to the interpretation of a particular Act. Where this Act has been adopted by Hong Kong as an Ordinance these cases may provide significant precedents for interpretation by Hong Kong courts on the meaning of the provisions of particular Ordinances. *Halsbury's Statutes* also allows you to find legislation relevant to a particular topic when you do not know the titles of the legislation. You can do this by consulting the extensive and consolidated subject index.

Case Law

Hong Kong

5.06 — Unlike ordinances, cases do not have titles that reveal their content. Their titles refer to the parties. By looking at the title of the case, we may be able to determine which party is plaintiff or defendant, appellant or respondent, but usually little more. The citation of the case follows its title and this refers to the law report in which the case can be found, the year of its publication and the page number. For example, in *Yuen Tam-wan v. Ho Chan Yuet-lan and Another* [1995] 1 HKLR 280 (see p. 57), the parties are Yuen Tam-wan, Ho Chan Yuet-lan and one other unnamed person. The case was reported in 1995 in the first volume of the Hong Kong Law Reports and begins at page 280. This is the traditional form of common law citation and occurs in other jurisdictions such as England, Australia and Canada. It is here that we will find out most things we might need to know about the case.

Accuracy in referencing a citation is vital because the smallest detail may be significant. Any mistake may cause difficulty in finding the case. Even the bracketing is significant; the use of [ ] around the year of the case report showing the year of reporting, while ( ) around the year shows that in that series the volumes are distinguished first by a volume number, rather than year.

If you know the citation then you can easily find the case, provided you have access to a library that holds the relevant series and you can interpret the citation. You should note that cases may appear in more than one series and, therefore, can have several citations. This is not so much the case for Hong Kong, which only has two principal law reports, but is particularly true for England. The case index in textbooks on the topic will usually provide you with alternative case citations if they exist, *e.g. R. v. Stone and Dobinson* [1977] QB 354, [1977] 2 All ER 341, [1977] 2 WLR 169, 141 JP 354, 121 Sol Jo 83, 64 Cr App Rep 186, C.A. You should be careful that you consult the correct report of the case. If the matter went on appeal there may be reports of the decision at first instance, and one or more appeals. It is most likely that you will only be interested in the last decision. Let's look at the following example from Findlay, Howarth and Dobinson, *Criminal Law in Hong Kong: Cases and Commentary* (2nd ed., 1996, Butterworths, Asia).

Ko Chi-yuen, [1993] 2 HKCLR 101, [1994] 2 HKCLR 65

In this example the first citation is the report of the initial hearing of the case in the High Court (now Court of First Instance), while the second is the Court of Appeal's decision.

If you are looking for cases on a particular topic, but do not have case names or citations to work from, it would *not* be productive to go through every volume of even one series of law reports searching for cases on the topic. A quicker approach would be to refer to the consolidated index of the particular series of law reports you are researching. You could also consult a law digest (these are discussed later in this chapter) to see what cases are listed under your topic. Both methods will provide you with a list of citations (the digest might also provide a brief summary of the case). You can now look up the case. Once into the case you will usually find a list of previous cases that are authorities on the topic. These can also be consulted in order to understand the precedent "history" of the case.

Having found your case, and before reading the entire report, you might want initially to determine whether it is relevant to the topic you are researching. Parts of the case report can assist you to do this. To demonstrate what has already been discussed let's look at the case of *Yuen Tam-wan* cited above.

First, there are numbers running down the left side of each page. These are the line numbers of the report and are important referencing tools for locating specific parts of the judgment. Next, we can see a list of parties. Two of these, Yuen Tam-wan and Ho Chan Yuet-lan were in the original citation, but the third, Ho Kai-hung, was not. In order, Ho Chan Yuet-lan is described as Petitioner and 1st Respondent, Ho Kai-hung as 1st and 2nd Respondent and Yuen Tam-wan as 2nd Respondent and Appellant. To the untrained eye this would appear very confusing and would require further reading to understand what has happened. What this indicates is that there have already been some legal proceedings and the initial status of each party was in accordance with what is

280

Ho Chan Yuet-lan	Petitioner (1st Respondent)
AND	
Ho Kai-hung	1st Respondent (2nd Respondent)
and	
Yuen Tam-wan	2nd Respondent (Appellant)

(Court of Appeal)
(Civil Appeal No. 34 of 1995)

Litton, V.-P., Bokhary, J. A. and Sears, J.
26th April 1995.

Family law—power of court to set aside disposition of property made to defeat claim for financial provision—whether transfer of undivided half-share in property amounted to such a disposition—Matrimonial Proceedings and Property Ordinance (*Cap*. 192), s. 17 (1) (b).

Property law—mortgage—where co-habitant made no contribution to purchase price or mortgage repayments of property registered in joint names, resulting trust arises.

Trusts—resulting trust—no evidence of arrangement or understanding between the parties that the co-habitant should acquire a beneficial interest in property registered in joint names—co-habitant made no contribution to purchase price or mortgage repayments.

The first respondent ("the husband") and the petitioner ("the wife") were married in China in 1950. In 1962 the husband came alone to Hong Kong and from 1969, he cohabitated with the second respondent ("Madam Yuen).

In May 1983 the husband and Madam Yuen purchased a property and were registered as joint owners. The husband, Madam Yuen and their three children lived in the premises until the husband left in 1992. Of the purchase price of $200,000, $140,000 was provided by Madam Yuen's mother with the balance raised on a bank mortgage. There was no evidence that the any part of the sum provided by Madam Yuen's mother was intended as a gift to the husband. Furthermore, although the husband contributed to the household expenses, there was no evidence controverting Madam Yuen's evidence that she had discharged the mortgage loan by monthly payments.

The wife came to Hong Kong in December 1988 and in February 1989, the husband gifted an undivided half-share in the property to Madam Yuen, making her the sole registered owner. The disposition was set aside by an order dated 19th August 1994, on the ground that the transaction was intended to defeat the claims of the wife against the husband for financial provision. Madam Yuen appealed.

Held

1. **The husband had made no contribution towards the purchase of the property or the discharge of the bank mortgage. (See p. 285, lines 34–40.) Hence the court inferred that the common intention of the parties was that the husband held his half-share in trust for Madam Yuen from the time of acquisition. (See p. 285, lines 41–43.)** *Lloyds Bank Plc. v. Rosset* **[1991] 1 AC 107 applied.**
2. **The disposition of the undivided half-share was the assignment of a bare legal estate and not a disposition falling within s. 17 (1) (b) of the Matrimonial Proceedings Ordinance (*Cap.* 192). (See p. 285, lines 43–45 and p. 286, lines 1–2.)**

Appeal allowed.

C. Y. Li, instructed by W. K. To & Co., for the appellant.
Miss E. Longmore, instructed by Fairbairn Catley Low & Kong, for 1st respondent.
2nd respondent is absent.

Case cited in the judgment:

Lloyds Bank Plc. v. Rosset [1991] 1 AC 107, [1990] 2 WLR 867, [1990] 1 All ER 1111

Litton, V.-P.:

There are three parties involved in this appeal: Madam Ho Chan Yuet-lan (the wife), Mr Ho Kai-hung (the husband) and Madam Yuen Tam-wan (madam Yuen). It concerns an undivided half-share in a property at Cheung Chau known as the G/F, 22 Tai San Street, Cheung Chau New Territories purchased in May 1983 in the names of the husband and madam Yuen as joint owners. By a deed of gift dated 11th February 1989, and registered in March 1989, the husband transferred that undivided half-share to madam Yuen, making her the sole registered owner.

By an order dated 19th August 1994 His Honour Judge Surman, in exercise of his powers under s. 17 (1) (b) of the Matrimonial Proceedings and Property Ordinance, set aside that the disposition on the ground that the transaction was intended to defeat the claims of the wife against the husband for financial provision in matrimonial proceedings brought by her. Madam Yuen, being aggrieved with that order, now appeals.

Background

The husband and wife were married in China in 1950. In early 1962 the husband came alone to Hong Kong, leaving the wife in China. From 1969 onwards he cohabited with madam Yuen and they have three children. In May 1983 the property was purchased in the joint names of the husband and madam Yuen. The husband carried on a small business there making quilts.

not in brackets. In the current case, their status has changed and this is reflected by what is in the brackets. By this we can determine that Ho Chan Yuet-lan initially brought a petition against Ho Kai-hung and Yuen Tam-wan. The use of the word "petitioner" would also indicate to the trained lawyer that this was a family law matter involving a marriage. The titles in brackets would then indicate that Yuen Tam-wan did not accept the first decision of the court and has now appealed.

This is confirmed by the next reference in the title, which tells us that this is a case heard by the Court of Appeal and that it was Civil Appeal No. 34 of 1995. Next is the list of judges who heard the case. These were Litton V.-P., Bokhary J. A. and Sears J. The letters after their names indicate their judicial status, Litton being Vice-President of the Court of Appeal, Bokhary a Justice of Appeal and Sears a Justice of the Supreme Court. As mentioned in Chapter 4, the Court of Appeal usually sits with a panel of three judges. The date, April 26, 1995, indicates the date on which the case was actually heard.

The next part provides some "catchwords" for the case. This is an important section that will alert you to whether or not this case is initially relevant to your topic of research. These tell us quite a lot about the case, which in our situation concerns matters of family law, property law and trusts. Next is a summary of the facts, which provides a brief history of how this case has come before the Court of Appeal.

This is then followed by a summary of the principal holdings, which is in bold type. This is known as the *Held* section. This is an extremely important part of the case report as it gives a summary of what was decided by the court and why it decided in this way. As discussed in Chapter 4, it is the "why" component which is the *ratio* of the case and could stand as precedent for subsequent, similar cases. In part 1 of the Held section, it is also important to note that the Court of Appeal has *applied* another case in coming to its decision. This is the English case of *Lloyds Bank Plc v. Rosset* [1991] 1 A.C. 107. This is an example of the operations of precedent as discussed earlier in Chapter 4. In part 2 of the Held section, it is stated that the disposition in the case was not a disposition that fell within the meaning of section 17 (1) (b) of the Matrimonial Proceedings Ordinance (Cap 192). This is an example of the court's application of one form of statutory interpretation. Statutory interpretation and the doctrine of precedent are discussed in detail in Chapter 7.

We are then told that the appeal was allowed, followed by the names of the barristers and solicitors who represented each of the parties. Next comes the cases cited section which contains a list of cases (in this instance only one) referred to in the judgment. This is an important part of any case report as it allows you to access a number of other cases that may be relevant to the areas of law you are researching.

All of the above is designated as the report's *headnote*. You should be cautious, however, in simply relying on what is said in the headnote. It is only the whole judgment that contains the written record of what was actually said by the judge or judges. The headnote is something that has been written by someone employed by the publishers of the case reports. In this regard, it is this person not the judge who is stating why the case was decided in the way it was. The headnote is extremely useful but you should always read the entire judgment and form your own conclusions of what is the *ratio* of the case.

Following the headnote are the original decisions as written by the court. In our situation, we see the beginning of the judgment by Litton V.-P. In the Court of Appeal it is usually the first judgment that is the most important. Indeed, if we were to read the report fully we would find that both Bokhary J. and Sears J. simply agreed with the judgment of Litton J.

5.07 — Law Reports — Set out below is a list of all the law report collections of Hong Kong cases. These are:

(a) Hong Kong Cases (HKC)
(b) Hong Kong Criminal Law Reports (HKCLR)—from 1992
(c) Hong Kong District Court Law Reports (HKDCLR)
(d) Hong Kong Inland Revenue Board of Review Decisions (IRBRD)
(e) Hong Kong Lands Tribunal Law Reports (HKLTR)
(f) Hong Kong Law Reports (HKLR)—from 1905 monthly volumes which include Hong Kong Law Reports, Hong Kong Criminal Law Reports and Hong Kong District Court Law Reports, which are all bound separately in annual volumes.
(g) Hong Kong Public Law Reports (HKPLR)
(h) Hong Kong Tax Cases (HKTC)
(i) Unreported Cases of the Supreme Court of Hong Kong—kept in files according to year and case number.

China

5.08 — China is not a common law jurisdiction and its approach to the application of legal principles is not affected by the doctrine of precedent in the same way as in Hong Kong. Just as Chinese legislation is important to the law student or legal practitioner in Hong Kong, however, so are Chinese cases. Apart from newspaper reports, there is only one source of Chinese cases in English. These are contained in the annual volumes of the China Law Reports (CLR). There are three volumes covering criminal, civil and administrative law. These case reports do not contain judicial interpretation and application of legal principle but are fundamentally summaries of the facts and judgment. They do, however, provide a useful insight into the Chinese judicial system.

Interpretations and directions to the courts can be found in the Bulletins of the Supreme People's Court of the People's Republic of China. This series contains answers by the Supreme Court to questions on law asked by the lower People's Courts, general directions by the Supreme Court to the lower People's Courts on the application of laws and punishments and some important cases. English translations of important parts of the Bulletin have been included in the volumes of the China Law Reports.

England

5.09 — English cases remain important to the study and practice of law in Hong Kong. While the jurisdictional connection no longer exists, the decisions of the House of Lords, Privy Council and Court of Appeal are likely to have a significant persuasive effect on Hong Kong courts in the future. Decisions of these three superior English Courts on the interpretation and application of common law principles remain important decisions that may be followed by the Hong Kong Courts. Similarly, English decisions concerning the interpretation of legislation that had been previously copied by Hong Kong prior to June 30, 1997, may also remain important to the deliberations of Hong Kong Courts in the Special Administrative Region.

The main sources of English case law and their citations are Appeal Cases (A.C.), Chancery Division (Ch.), Family Division (Fam.), Queens Bench Division (Q.B.), Weekly Law Reports, (W.L.R.) and All England Law Reports (All E.R.). If we know the name of the English case we can also consult other primary sources. These include the *Current Law Case Citator*, *The Digest*, and *Halsbury's Laws*.

Secondary or Literary Sources

5.10 — Law books which stock the shelves of the library can be distinguished in terms of the material that they contain and whether they have any authoritative status. As discussed above, some law books contain law in a primary source form, such as the Laws of Hong Kong and the Hong Kong Law Reports, and are, therefore, authoritative in nature. Secondary or literary sources can be described on the other hand as *books about law* and have no authority. The main literary sources for law include:

(a) Legal encyclopedias and digests
(b) Textbooks
(c) Journals, periodicals and newspapers
(d) Computerised information systems

Legal Encyclopedias and Digests

5.11 — At present, Hong Kong is not well served by local legal encyclopedias. This position is changing quickly, however, with the gradual release of the volumes of *Hong Kong Halsbury*. All volumes of this collection, which mirrors its English counterpart (discussed below), should be available around the end of 2000. Current and previous collections include the *Hong Kong Law Digest* and *Addison's Digests*. *Addison's Digests* consist of case summaries of published and unpublished cases. To find case law on a particular topic, these Digests provide subject indexes. Unfortunately, the volumes of Addison's criminal case law are only up to date to 1989 and its civil case law to 1991. We can update Addison by using the *Hong Kong Law Digest* (HKLD). This series began in 1985 under the title *Hong Kong Current Law*. It is a monthly series and provides details of recent cases, legislation and the amounts of damages awarded in civil matters. Each volume also contains a cumulative subject index, the December issue containing a subject index for the whole year. To date there has been no consolidated index. In association with the HKLD, the *Hong Kong Law Year Book* provides case law and legislative developments, indexed by subject, for each year (since 1985).

While Hong Kong is not well served by legal encyclopedias, the two English collections *Halsbury's Laws* and *Current Law* provide an excellent means for researching English case and statute law on a particular topic. As discussed in Chapters 4 and 6, common law has evolved through the judgments of cases heard over many hundreds of years. To understand a principle of common law, therefore, we may wish to trace its development through those judgments. You might also want to research how a particular case has been dealt with by later cases. Has it been followed by later courts or has a court distinguished or overruled it? *Halsbury* facilitates such research as demonstrated by the following example.

Researching a Case Using the Digests

5.12 — Let's look again at the examples mentioned at the end of Chapter 4. In the first case a dispute has arisen between Mr Chan and his neighbour, Mr Cheung, over a fire that has damaged Mr Cheung's property caused by sparks from welding being done by Mr Chan. In the second case there has been another fire, this time starting in the premises of Mr Leung. His neighbour, Mr Lee's property has been subsequently damaged by smoke and water used to extinguish the fire. Both neighbours have suffered financial loss owing to this damage. Are Mr Chan and Mr Leung liable for compensating their neighbour for this loss? How would we go about finding the law to help answer this question?

By using the word "neighbour" as your key word you could look at *Halbury's Consolidated Index*. Here you would find the reference 34 29. The volumes of *Halsbury* are numbered and divided into paragraphs. This will tell you that what you are looking for is located in volume 34, paragraph 29. By looking up this reference you would find your paragraph entitled "Duty to Neighbours", which comes under the general heading of "Negligence". This section tells us that one neighbour has a duty to take reasonable care to prevent damage to persons or property on adjoining premises and this seems relevant to our research. Further down the paragraph, it states that "an occupier is also liable for damage caused to his neighbours by fire which he has negligently caused or allowed to spread . . .". There is a footnote to this section of the text. This is footnote 7, which cites the case of *Mulholland and Ted Ltd v. Baker* [1939] 3 All E.R. 253. It also says that there may also be liability in such circumstances under the rule in *Rylands v. Fletcher* (1868) LR 3 H.L. 330, which is discussed in paragraph 339. Paragraph 339 is entitled "The Rule in *Rylands v. Fletcher*". This tells us that those who bring onto and keep anything on their land that is likely to do mischief if it escapes are liable for damage to neighbouring properties if it does escape. Further on it says that the rule only applies to a non-natural use of the land. The concept of non-natural use is then discussed in paragraph 340. There it is said that there is no precise definition of the term but it will be non-natural use if it is not the ordinary use of the land or it is not proper use that is of general benefit to the community. In paragraph 341, fire is said to be something likely to do mischief. The concept of escape is then discussed in paragraph 342, which says that the rule in *Rylands v. Fletcher* only applies where the thing has escaped and that this means that it has escaped "from a place where the defendant has occupation or control over land to a place which is outside his occupation or control."

The main volumes of *Halsbury*, however, are not up to date. What, then, is the most recent case law on this area? The next place to look is the most recent volume of the Cumulative Supplement. Our reference points are volume 34, paragraphs 29 and 339–342. In the Cumulative Supplement there are no helpful references under paragraph 29. Under paragraph 339, however, there is reference to the case of *Cambridge Water Co. Ltd. v. Eastern Counties Leather plc* [1994] 1 All E.R. 53. The note goes on to say that foreseeability of damage is a prerequisite of any liability under the *Rylands v. Fletcher* rule.

What about the position in Hong Kong? The first place to look would be *Addison Civil Cases*. By using the subject index of the various volumes, we would find the following reference "Negligence—see Tort". Unfortunately, there is no Cumulative Index to *Addison*, so we have to work our way laboriously through the whole Tort section in each volume. This search would reveal two references under the heading "the rule in *Rylands v. Fletcher*" and two cases are referred to. The first is the case of *Leeth & Co. Ltd. and Others v. Mack & Co. (Freight Forwarders) Ltd. and Others* [1978] HKLR 333 and the second, *Wayfoong Credit Ltd. and Others v. Tsui Siu-man T/A Wilsons Plastics Manufactory* [1984] HKLR 259. Each case is summarised.

In *Leeth & Co.*, the facts concerned sparks caused by welding, which caused a fire on an adjoining property. In *Wayfoong*, there was another fire that had started in the premises of the defendant. The fire had been made worse by the accumulation of plastics stored by the defendant, the associated heat, smoke and water (used to extinguish the fire) causing damage to the plaintiff's adjoining property. Both cases are important in what they say about the application of *Rylands v. Fletcher*, but more importantly they are very similar to the cases of Mr Chan and Mr Leung. In these circumstances, you would be correct in concluding that they would be important to the determination of the liability of Mr Chan and Mr Leung.

Wayfoong was reported in 1984 but, according to *Addison*, was the most recent case on this topic as at 1991. We would still need to determine, however, whether there have been any further relevant court decisions since then. As mentioned, *Addison* can be updated using the volumes of the *Hong Kong Law Digest*. As there is no cumulative index, this would again involve a laborious volume by volume search, the end result being that no more recent decisions would be located.

Textbooks

5.13 — You could have found this information much more easily, however, had you gone straight to the textbook *The Law of Tort in Hong*

Kong by D. K. Srivastava and A. D. Tennekone (Butterworths, Asia, 1995). Textbooks are extremely useful secondary sources and in some cases what they say may even be cited by courts in their judgments. We can divide them into two types: academic and practitioner, although this does not necessarily mean they are mutually exclusive or that one group would not refer to the other's textbooks. This distinction is primarily concerned with the purpose for which they are written. They are, however, the views and opinions only of the authors. What is said, for example, about the importance or meaning of a case must be read in this light and, as mentioned earlier, it is only the case itself that has authoritative status. For those studying or practising law, textbooks are a useful starting point but should not be used as a substitute for reading the actual case or legislation. Even casebooks only provide selected extracts from judgments or legislation.

In Hong Kong, there are what we would call the basic textbooks, covering such topics as tort (see above), contract, company law, property law, evidence and criminal law, as well as more specialist texts on subjects such as banking. There are also practitioner texts (quite often in loose-leaf format) on such things as criminal and civil litigation, taxation and sentencing. Apart from these publications, there are also numerous books about the law or a particular legal issue. These may also be useful sources for finding law on a particular or related topic, *e.g.* human rights.

Law libraries will also hold textbooks and other books which discuss the law in other jurisdictions, *e.g.* England, Australia, the USA and Canada. These too are important sources of law which a student or practitioner of law might wish to access and use.

Journals and Periodicals

5.14 — What has been said about legal texts and law related books above can also be used to describe legal journals and periodicals. Some can be described as mainly academic while others are primarily for the legal practitioner. They are extremely useful sources of law as the articles that make up the journal or periodical are often the result of detailed and in-depth research on a specific topic or area of law (see for example Dobinson, I. "Bribery Offences" *The Employment Report* 1993 1(3) 373–384).

There are a number of Hong Kong-based law journals. These include the *Asia Pacific Law Review*, the *Journal of Chinese and Comparative Law*, the *Hong Kong Law Journal*, the *Hong Kong Student Law Review* and the *Asian Commercial Law Review*. These publications contain material specific to Hong Kong, China and other jurisdictions in the region. The main practitioner periodical is the *New Gazette*. There are also other local journals and periodicals that contain legal articles as well as other non-law material, *e.g. The Employment Report*.

There are literally thousands of law journals published in the various jurisdictions around the world. Law libraries will subscribe to a limited number of these. Not surprisingly, Hong Kong law libraries place an emphasis on those published in other common law jurisdictions as well as certain areas of law, *e.g.* commercial law and international law.

Computerised Information Systems

5.15 — Given the amount of law and related information on this law, it is not surprising that the trend is toward computerised storage, updating and retrieval. A number of these systems have already been discussed, *e.g.* INFO/LAW (operated by the Hong Kong Legal Department), Law-On-Line (Law Faculty, Hong Kong University) and Chinese Law on CD-ROM.

The most well-known computerised primary law source, however, is *Lexis*. This system allows for the retrieval of the full text of legislation and cases from a number of jurisdictions around the world, including Hong Kong and China. It also allows the user to search specific topics by adopting a keyword(s) approach. Apart from legislation and cases, this system also includes journals, periodicals and newspapers.

The law reports, *Hong Kong Cases*, and *Hong Kong Law Digest* are also available on CD-ROM and it is proposed that *Hong Kong Halsbury* will eventually be available in this form. Other computerised secondary source data bases include the Index to Legal Periodicals (CD-ROM) and the Legal Journals Index (CD-ROM). Apart from these specific law journal databases, there are many other non-law collections that may contain law related articles (see, for example, the Social Science Index (CD-ROM)). Finally, the Internet and especially the World-Wide Web also allow you to search many other collections of legal materials around the world.

SIX

HOW LAW IS ADMINISTERED

6.01 — Every society creates for itself processes for resolving disputes, or has those processes imposed from outside. Modern civilised communities have procedures for dealing with disputes between individuals and also between individuals and the community. There is a better chance of order in a society if these processes are generally acceptable.

The Courts

6.02 — The processes described above include those operated by the courts. It is there that disputes that necessitate a legal resolution are dealt with. In settling such disputes in common law jurisdictions courts will:

(a) Apply and interpret legislation
(b) Apply and interpret common law principles

As mentioned in Chapter 4, it is through this process that the courts make law. Future courts may then be subsequently bound to follow such decisions. In this regard, precedent is said to be hierarchical, *i.e.* lower (*inferior*) courts are bound by the decisions of higher (*superior*) courts. Another way of classifying courts is whether the court is one of *first instance* or *appellate*. Courts may also be classified by their jurisdiction, *civil* or *criminal*.

Inferior and Superior—Courts and the judges who sit in them are ranked in a hierarchy. The doctrine of precedent holds that inferior courts are bound by the decisions of superior courts, and that courts will usually follow previous decisions of courts at the same level.

First Instance and Appellate—Courts of first instance (sometimes called *original courts*) hear and decide a case first. If, however, a party is dissatisfied with the decision of this court, it can appeal to a superior court in an attempt to have the original decision changed. Procedural rules (see Chapter 8) restrict a party's access to an appellate court. Students should be careful not to conclude that the terms inferior and superior are synonymous with first instance and appellate. Superior courts can be both courts of first instance and appellate courts, *e.g.* the Court of First Instance (the old High Court).

Civil and Criminal—Courts may also be divided by the kinds of legal dispute that they are empowered to hear. This is part of what is known as the court's jurisdiction. In some jurisdictions, *e.g.* England, specialist courts dealing only with certain areas of law have been established. This has not been the case in Hong Kong, however, although the Family Law Division of the District Court was first set up in 1972. There have been proposals for setting up specialist divisions of the Court of First Instance in the future, but at present the District Court and Court of First Instance hear a wide range of both civil and criminal cases.

The Hong Kong Court System

6.03 — The hierarchy of the Hong Kong court system is the Court of Final Appeal, the Court of Appeal, the Court of First Instance, the District Court and the Magistrates Court. There are also a number of tribunals attached to this court system. These are the Lands Tribunal,

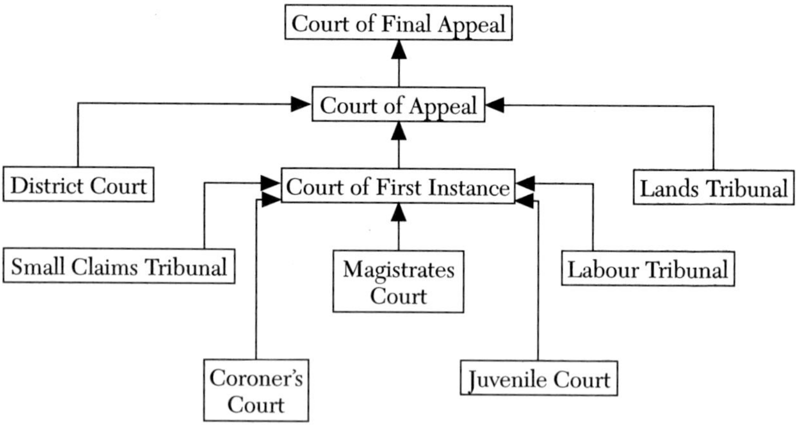

Hong Kongs Courts & Tribunals
(Showing Appeal Process)

Labour Tribunal and Small Claims Tribunal. A party dissatisfied with a ruling of one of these tribunals may appeal against its decision to either the Court of First Instance or Court of Appeal. Details of this will be discussed later.

This is essentially the same structure as existed before June 30, 1997 with the important exception of the establishment of the Court of Final Appeal to replace the Judicial Committee of the Privy Council. According to Article 19 of the Basic Law "The Hong Kong Special Administrative Region shall be vested with independent judicial power, including that of final adjudication." The courts have jurisdiction over all cases in the region except for those restrictions "imposed by the legal system and principles previously in force in Hong Kong . . ." The effect of these restrictions is discussed fully in Chapter 7.

The Basic Law (Section 4—The Judiciary) outlines the provisions relevant to structure, power and functions of the SAR courts. Article 81 details the hierarchical structure set out above and states that the judicial system previously in place will be maintained except for the Court of Final Appeal. In this sense, the jurisdictions and procedures of the courts remain the same. Trial by jury, for example, is maintained by Article 86. Article 85 confirms the principle of judicial independence, stating that the courts shall exercise their power independently, *free from any interference*.

Judges are appointed by the Chief Executive on the recommendation of an independent commission (Article 88) in much the same way as the Governor appointed judges who were recommended by the Judicial Services Commission. Both the Chief Justice of the Court of Final Appeal and the Chief Judge of the High Court are required to be Chinese citizens and permanent residents of the Hong Kong SAR (Article 90). Judges may also be removed by the Chief Executive on the recommendation of a specially convened tribunal (Article 89). In the case of the Chief Justice or Chief Judge both approval or removal must be endorsed by the Legislative Council and reported to the Standing Committee of the NPC. Magistrates are appointed and removed in the same way as they were prior to the changeover (Article 91). The appointment of a magistrate is similar to that of any other civil servant. The difference is that, in addition, magistrates are appointed under *warrant* which is a certification of their judicial authority.

The Court of Final Appeal

6.04 — This is the highest and final court of appeal in the judicial system. This Court replaced the Judicial Committee of the Privy Council, which was the court of final appeal for Hong Kong until June 30, 1997. One of the significant differences between the two courts is that the Court of Final Appeal is a court of the Hong Kong SAR, whereas the Judicial Committee is a court located in England that hears appeals from present and some former British colonies.

The court was established by the Court of Final Appeal Ordinance, passed in August 1995. By agreement with China, however, the court did not sit until after June 30, 1997. Under section 4, the Court is deemed not to have any jurisdiction to hear cases involving acts of state such as defence and foreign affairs. This limitation is in accordance with Article 13 of the Basic Law which states that Hong Kong's foreign affairs are the responsiblity of the Central People's Government. Apart from this restriction the Court has significant power and, in accordance with Article 158, it is empowered to interpret the Basic Law (this role will be discussed in more detail in Chapter 7).

A panel of five judges hears the cases brought before the Court of Final Appeal. Section 5 of the Ordinance states that the constitution of the Court shall include the Chief Justice, permanent judges and non-permanent judges. The Chief Executive appoints those who will be permanent judges. Non-permanent judges include Hong Kong judges (appointed in accordance with Article 88) as well as judges from common law countries overseas (see sections 7, 8 and 9). In accordance with section 16, the Court will be constituted by the Chief Justice, three permanent judges, one non-permanent Hong Kong judge or one non-permanent overseas judge.

Special permission called *leave* must be granted by the Court of Appeal or the Court of Final Appeal itself before an appeal can be heard. Like its predecessor, the Judicial Committee of the Privy Council, the Court of Final Appeal only hears matters involving questions of law that are of particular importance to Hong Kong, which will include the interpretation of the Basic Law.

Court of Appeal and Court of First Instance (High Court)

6.05 — The High Court (previously known as the Supreme Court) is an amalgamation of two courts, the Court of Appeal and the Court of First Instance (previously known as the High Court). The Court of Appeal hears both civil and criminal appeals arising from the Court of First Instance, District Court and Lands Tribunal. A panel of judges (usually three) hears such appeals only after leave has been granted by the court. All High Court judges are eligible to sit on the Court of Appeal, but some judges, the Judges of Appeal, sit only there. The Court of First

Instance has unlimited jurisdiction in both civil and criminal matters. It has original (first instance) jurisdiction in all civil matters involving damages, where the claim is for an amount in excess of $120,000. It also has exclusive jurisdiction over matters involving bankruptcy, company liquidation, adoption, probate and insanity certifications.

In criminal matters, the Court of First Instance tries the serious crimes of murder, manslaughter, rape, armed robbery and drug offences involving large quantities of dangerous drugs. Court proceedings in such cases do not start immediately in the Court of First Instance. Procedure requires that such matters be heard first by a Magistrates Court (committal proceedings). An accused, however, may waive the right to committal (section 80C Magistrates Ordinance (Cap 227)) and have the matter go straight to the Court of First Instance.

Criminal cases in the Court of First Instance are heard by a judge and a jury. The jury is usually made up of seven or nine randomly selected adult Hong Kong residents. Further aspects of the jury will be discussed later in this chapter.

The Court of First Instance also hears appeals from decisions of the magistrates courts, Labour and Small Claims Tribunals. Appeals are heard by a judge sitting alone, without a jury.

District Court

6.06 — The District Court has limited civil and criminal jurisdiction. It can hear claims for damages from $15,000 to $120,000. It will also hear actions for the recovery of land where the rateable value of the land or the annual rent is less than $100,000.

The court has wide jurisdiction in criminal cases, trying serious offences, with the exception of those which are within the exclusive jurisdiction of the Court of First Instance. It is limited, however, to a maximum penalty of seven years imprisonment. In a trial, the judge sits alone without a jury. There are no committal proceedings prior to a District Court trial.

Magistrates Court

6.07 — The Magistrates Courts are the originating courts for all criminal cases. Following an arrest, all offenders are taken first before a magistrate. At this time the question of bail is considered. A date will then be fixed for the offender to appear again before the magistrate. Most criminal cases are also tried by the Magistrates Courts, which also handle committal proceedings to the Court of First Instance. In all cases the magistrate is the sole decision-maker. The Court is restricted in its sentencing powers, being able to imprison an offender for up to two years (three in special circumstances) and impose a fine of no more than $10,000 unless a greater fine is specified by the legislation.

Gradually proceedings in all courts, though still mainly held in English, are more and more held in Chinese. This is particularly true in the Magistrates Court, but the number of trials in Chinese in both the District Court and Court of First Instance is also increasing.

Coroner's Court

6.08 — This special court inquires into the identity of unidentified deceased persons and determines (if possible) the cause of death where this has resulted from sudden and unexplained circumstances. In some cases, a coroner may utilise a jury of three persons. The findings of a coroner can lead to criminal proceedings, notably murder and manslaughter.

Juvenile Court

6.09 — Apart from homicide offences, the juvenile court deals with all criminal charges brought against children between the ages of seven and 16. Children over 16 (up to the age of 21) are dealt with as if they were adults, *i.e.* in the Magistrates Courts, District Court or Court of First Instance. There are also certain procedural rules to be considered in the trial of such children as well as their sentencing. Apart from this, the court hears matters involving the proper care and protection of children up to the age of 18. For example, children who are not being properly fed by their parents can be taken from them and put in the care of a foster family.

Tribunals

6.10 — In addition to the courts, there are three tribunals that form part of Hong Kong's judicial system. All three tribunals were established in the mid-1970s—mainly in order to provide a mechanism for the quick and efficient resolution of common legal disputes. The perceived advantages of the system are the informality of procedure (as compared to that required by the courts), a less rigid adherence to rules of evidence and a reduction in legal costs.

Labour Tribunal

6.11 — This tribunal deals with disputes between employers and employees, with special emphasis on the contract of employment. Typical disputes involve claims over wrongful dismissal, sickness and holiday pay and severance pay. It does not deal with cases involving physical injuries sustained at work, these being within the jurisdiction of the District Court or Court of First Instance. Proceedings are presided over by a government-appointed officer who is said to have expertise in such disputes. Most cases are heard in Chinese. No legal representation (barristers or solicitors) is allowed. Parties dissatisfied with a decision can appeal to the Court of First Instance.

Small Claims Tribunal

6.12 — This tribunal was established specifically to lighten the workload of the District Court in dealing with small monetary claims, particularly debts and damages. Its jurisdiction is currently restricted to amounts not exceeding $15,000. It is presided over by magistrates with no legal representation allowed. Most cases are heard in Chinese. Appeals are made to the Court of First Instance.

Lands Tribunal

6.13 — This tribunal has three principal functions. First, it deals with the determination of compensation where land has been compulsorily resumed by the government. A notable example of this was the compensation paid to the owners of the land resumed by the government for construction of the new Hong Kong airport at Chek Lap Kok. Second, it hears appeals from property owners against the determination of the rateable value of their property, and appeals from tenants against rent increases. Lastly, its work also includes a variety of determinations in relation to domestic premises under the Landlord and Tenant (Consolidation) Ordinance.

The tribunal consists of a legally qualified president and other officers appointed by the Chief Executive. Legal representation is allowed and cases are heard in English and Chinese. Appeals are made to the Court of Appeal.

Other Tribunals

6.14 — There are other tribunals in Hong Kong that can be said to have a quasi-judicial function. Two examples of these are the Inland Revenue Board of Review and the Immigration Tribunal. Both deal with appeals against decisions of the relevant commissioners regarding, for example, an income tax assessment and the refusal of a visa. Such tribunals, however, are not part of the judicial system. There is no right of appeal to a higher court: their decisions are said to be final. There is a right to seek judicial review by the Court of First Instance or the Court of Appeal, but this is limited to questions of law and the exercise of power of the tribunal itself. Even if an appellant is successful, the matter will be returned to the tribunal for consideration. It is appropriate to discuss these tribunals or review boards, together with bodies such as the Labour Tribunal, because in hearing the claims of individuals they decide questions of both fact and law. Further, their decisions are binding on the parties, *e.g.* both the Commissioner for Inland Revenue and a taxpayer in dispute over an income tax assessment, and, therefore, can be seen to be deciding legal disputes.

The Adversarial System

6.15 — One method of resolving legal disputes is to treat the opposing sides as *adversaries*. In a civil matter they are the plaintiff and the defendant, while in a criminal case they are the State and the accused. This is the system in all common law jurisdictions, with the judge or magistrate playing the role of a neutral umpire.

Such a system allows people to confront their accusers in court and requires the accuser to prove the case. The burden on the accuser, which differs in civil and criminal matters, is discussed in Chapter 8. Both parties are allowed legal representation and can call witnesses to give evidence in support of their case. In some cases, a party may be given legal aid. This service is provided by the Legal Aid Department and allows for Government-appointed lawyers to appear for a party at the Government's expense. There are numerous conditions attached to this, *e.g.* a financial means test. As previously stated, legal representation is precluded in some of the tribunals, *e.g.* the Small Claims Tribunal.

Through a process of examination and cross-examination of witnesses and the placing of other evidence before the court, it is believed that the truth can be tested and established. Having heard all the evidence, a judge or jury can then decide the guilt or innocence of an accused, for example, or the liability for damages of a defendant.

Judges and Juries

6.16 — Legal disputes are all about questions of law and fact. In a case of attempted theft, whether the accused had the required guilty intention (*mens rea*) to steal is a question of fact, while whether putting a hand in an empty pocket amounts to attempt is a question of law. In an action for breach of contract, whether one party failed to fulfill a term is a question of fact, while whether such a term is a condition or a warranty is a question of law.

In medieval times the English legal system adopted a procedure whereby questions of law were decided by a judge, and questions of fact by a jury. The jury was selected from the local citizens. This was the case for both criminal and civil matters. The principle became that the judge would *direct* the jury as to the law. The jury would then apply the rules of law to the facts that they found proved.

Today in Hong Kong, juries are used only in original criminal proceedings in the Court of First Instance and (very rarely) in defamation. The vast majority of criminal matters (District and Magistrates Courts) and virtually all civil cases (Court of First Instance and District Court) are presided over by a single judge. Accordingly, the judge or magistrate is the sole arbiter of both fact and law. The role of the jury has shrunk for a number of reasons. First, the division of crimes into groups such as indictable and summary offences (see Chapter 8 for a discussion of the distinction) has resulted in less serious offences (summary offences) being treated as not warranting a jury trial. Magistrates are seen as quite capable of deciding such cases alone. A quicker, cheaper and more efficient means of disposal of such offences in the District Court was another motivating factor.

Practical considerations, such as length of hearing and shortage of qualified jurors, ended the use of juries in ordinary civil matters and reduced them drastically in criminal trials. It is unreasonable to expect people to give their time to a case that could take many weeks. The payment given to jurors also increases the overall cost of the process.

The Jury in Hong Kong

6.17 — In 1989, the jury system in Hong Kong was the subject of a detailed inquiry and analysis (Duff, P., Findlay, M., Howarth, C., and

Chan T. F., *Juries: A Hong Kong Perspective* (Hong Kong University Press, 1992)). It was found (at p. 34):

> "In theory, the jury exists in order to ascertain what the facts are, and then to determine on the basis of them, whether the defendant is guilty of the crime as charged. The ideology is that the jury is made up of a group of ordinary people who apply their knowledge of the world and experiences in the community to courtroom decisions. Ever since the jury was given breath in Hong Kong, however, there has been a very particular, and some may say peculiar, definition of the 'ordinary person' who becomes the ordinary juror in this territory."

Those selected for jury service in Hong Kong must be between the ages of 21 and 65, be resident within the colony, must not suffer from deafness, blindness or any other infirmity and must have a standard of English that will enable them to understand the proceedings in court (Jury Ordinance, s. 4). The Immigration Department maintains a List of Common Jurors from which jury members are selected.

The language requirement for jury selection is significant. In practice, residents must have obtained at least a Form 6 level of English. This, together with exemptions from jury service (discussed later), has resulted in only 170,000 residents out of a total population of over six million being eligible for jury service. Further to this, a large percentage of juries are made up of non-Chinese residents and represent mainly the wealthy elite of Hong Kong.

Apart from the language requirement, the number of eligible jurors is further reduced by those who are either exempt or disqualified. Those exempt include all judges, magistrates, coroners, barristers, solicitors (only those admitted in Hong Kong), barristers' clerks, court clerks and other court staff involved in the day-to-day administration of the courts, clergy, monks, nuns, the mentally ill, members of the armed forces, doctors and people of similar professions. This list is quite standard for most jurisdictions where juries are used, but in Hong Kong it is expanded by the exemption of newspaper editors, full-time students, pilots and crew of passenger and commercial aircraft, masters and crew of ships, harbour pilots, navigators and wireless operators. Even the wives of Supreme Court judges cannot serve as jurors.

The result of the language requirement, exemptions and exclusions has been to reduce significantly the pool of available jurors. To ease the problem, the number of jurors in a Court of First Instance criminal trial is only seven or sometimes nine persons compared with the traditional 12 in England.

Empanelling the Jury

6.18 — Even if you are called to jury service, this does not mean that you will necessarily be a member of a jury that hears a case. Through a system of *challenges* by the defendant and the prosecution, and the *standing by* of jurors by the prosecution, a total prospective pool of approximately 20 (the jury in waiting) is reduced to the seven or nine jurors who are actually chosen to hear the case.

Directing the Jury

6.19 — "The jury is seen as being able to weigh up the facts presented to them, decide which witnesses to believe and which to doubt, to apply their own experience to judge whether certain events were probable or possible, and to determine whether the defendant's story is believable or not." (Duff *et al.*, 1992, p. 35)

In determining a defendant's guilt or innocence a jury should apply the law, as directed by the judge, to its findings of fact. Such directions may be specific, *e.g.* the necessary requirements for the *mens rea* of murder, or general, *e.g.* that the prosecution must have proved its case against the defendant "beyond reasonable doubt", failure to do so resulting in an acquittal.

Misdirection of a jury by a judge is the most common ground for an appeal from the Court of First Instance to the Court of Appeal. In Chapter 8, we will deal with the legal procedure for appeals in detail, but the following example demonstrates how a jury can be misdirected and how this forms the basis for an appeal.

In *Wong Tak Sing v. R.* [1989] 2 HKC 94, the accused appealed against his conviction for murder on the ground that the trial judge had misdirected the jury on the required *mens rea* for murder. In allowing the appeal, and substituting a verdict of manslaughter, the Court of Appeal outlined the misdirection by the High Court (now Court of First Instance) and what a correct direction in such cases should be.

In referring to the direction by the trial judge, Silke J. stated:

> "Then, a little further down at that page, he said this:
>
>> 'Now, members of the jury, in carrying out that act, . . . what do you believe his intention was? Was the *probable consequence* of his action one of causing her grievous bodily harm or even killing her?

> If it was, if that was his intent and you are satisfied of that, then the Crown has proved the necessary intent to have the defendant convicted of murder.' [Emphasis supplied]

This was an unfortunate direction. It ignored the advice given in *R. v. Moloney* [1985] A.C. 905 where Lord Bridge of Harwich said at page 926:

> 'The golden rule should be that, when directing a jury on the mental element necessary in a crime of specific intent, the jury should avoid an elaboration or paraphrase of what is meant by intent, and leave it to the jury's good sense to decide whether the accused acted with the necessary intent, unless the judge is convinced that, on the facts and having regard to the way the case has been presented to the jury in evidence and argument, some further explanation or elaboration is strictly necessary to avoid misunderstanding. In trials for murder or wounding with intent, I find it very difficult to visualise a case where any such explanation or elaboration could be required, if the offence consisted of a direct attack on the victim with a weapon, except possibly the case where the accused shot at A and killed B, which any first year law student could explain to a jury in the simplest of terms. Even where the death results indirectly from the act of the accused, I believe the cases that will call for a direction by reference to foresight of consequences will be of extremely rare occurrence.'

This was not, on any footing, a case which might require a direction on foresight of consequences. *Moloney*, explained in *R v. Hancock and Shankland* [1986] A.C. 455 and *R. v. Nedrick* [1986] 1 W.L.R. 1025 was, as were the others, a case of an indirect act. Here there was a direct attack with a weapon, whether or not in the first instance movement of her neck by the girl may have resulted in the knife's penetrating her. The direction was quite unnecessary. But, once a direction of this nature is given, then it must be given properly. This was not. What concerns me is that in the perfectly proper directions both earlier and later in the summing up, which emphasised the word 'intent', that word may have become coloured in the minds of the jury by the passage I have just cited. If they believed that the Applicant thought that the *probable consequence* of his action would be to cause the girl grievous bodily harm or even killing her then, they were told, in effect, that that was his intent. This is wrong.

While the expression 'natural consequences' was used in *Moloney* this, it was made clear, meant that the consequences must be 'overwhelming'. In *Hancock and Shankland* the expression 'high probability' was used which became, in *Nedrick* 'virtually certain'—and this is now the correct phrase and emphasis if a direction on foresight is to be given at all. A jury should be told that a result is intended when it is the doer's purpose and they should be directed, if necessary, that they may infer that a result is intended, though it is not desired, when the result is a virtually certain consequence of the act and the doer knows that it is a virtually certain consequence (pp. 100–1)."

Alternative Dispute Resolution

6.20 — Apart from courts and tribunals, there are other methods of dispute resolution. These include arbitration, mediation or conciliation, and negotiation.

Arbitration

6. 21 — Arbitration has developed as the most formal alternative method of dispute resolution. It involves the appointment of a third party to act as an arbitrator. The agreement to submit a dispute to arbitration may be before it happens—by an arbitration clause in a contract—or after. The parties will usually be legally represented and will call witnesses who are then subject to examination and cross-examination. The rules of procedure and evidence will be at the parties' discretion and the arbitrator's award will normally be final.

Arbitrations often involve contractual disputes between parties. In the case of a delay in the completion of a building, for example, an arbitrator may be called upon to decide who bears the responsibility for the delay and thereafter make an award in the form of monetary compensation.

In Hong Kong, arbitrations often take place in the Hong Kong International Arbitration Centre. This Centre deals with a wide variety of both domestic and international disputes. The centre provides a venue for the hearing of the dispute as well as a panel of expert arbitrators from which the parties may choose.

Arbitration is as expensive as litigation (in some cases more so), but is usually speedier. The arbitrator may be an expert in the field, *e.g.* an architect, rather than a lawyer. The proceedings, unlike litigation, can also be kept secret.

Mediation and Conciliation

6.22 — In this process a neutral third party is appointed to try to achieve a resolution of the dispute without having to resort to the courts or tribunals. In Hong Kong, this process is often used in disputes involving family law, rental disputes in public housing and increasingly in building construction disputes.

An example of family law mediation is that undertaken by the Hong Kong Marriage Advisory Council, while the Housing Authority's Rating and Valuation Department offers an informal mediation service for rent disputes. At this stage mediation processes in Hong Kong are informal and voluntary. New methods of mediation are constantly devised, with the advantages of informality, reduction of hostility and the possibility of compromise.

Conciliation and mediation are usually synonymous in Hong Kong but, elsewhere, there are some who draw the distinction that a conciliator facilitates the discussions and communications between the parties so that they, themselves, can reach a mutually agreed resolution. In other countries, conciliation in labour disputes, for example claims for wage increases, is compulsory before parties can resort to a more formal process or employees go on strike. In Hong Kong, however, the practice is voluntary and has largely arisen out of the practices of the Labour Department. The Labour Relations Service, for example, is now the predominant first stage in most labour disputes. As a member of GATT (General Agreement on Tariffs and Trade), Hong Kong can also make use of that international organisation's Panels of Conciliation for the settling of certain overseas commercial disputes.

Negotiation

6.23 — The parties in a commercial dispute will usually try to negotiate a settlement and thus avoid the costs of lengthy litigation. Some form of a voluntary informal process, involving the parties or their legal representatives, will be attempted to resolve the dispute. The difference between negotiation and the other main forms of alternative dispute resolution is that it does not involve a third party.

Negotiation also has significance for the law in foreign affairs. The negotiated Sino-British Joint Declaration in 1984, for example, established the processes for the return of Hong Kong to China on July 1, 1997.

Ombudsman and Others

6.24 — Other important examples of alternative approaches to dispute resolution in Hong Kong include the office of the Commissioner for Administrative Complaints, often called "the Ombudsman", which hears complaints from persons concerning the actions of the various Government Departments; and the Social Security Appeal Board which hears appeals from persons dissatisfied with decisions regarding the payment of or eligibility for social welfare.

While the development of alternative dispute resolution has taken place mostly in the area of civil law, it is also worth noting some examples involving criminal offences. The cautioning of juveniles by police, for example, is a formal process that seeks to avoid recourse to a criminal trial.

SEVEN

HOW LAW IS APPLIED

7.01 — As stated in Chapter 5, it is the judges who play the pivotal role in the development of the law through the processes of statutory interpretation and precedent. The application of the law, therefore, relies upon the exercise of judicial discretion in the decision making process. It was noted, however, that such discretion is not unlimited. A District Court judge, for example, is bound by the rules of precedent to follow a decision of the Court of Appeal. Certain rules of statutory interpretation have also been developed by higher courts over the years to guide judges in the exercise of their discretion to interpret the law and legal principles. The aim of this chapter is to describe these rules and to analyse more fully the operation of precedent.

Statutory Interpretation

7.02 — Many students might assume that because of the different process through which it arises legislation should be far less difficult to interpret than case law. By simply looking up and reading the relevant section of the ordinance, for instance, we should understand the meaning of the written word, and thereby know the law. In Chapter 5, however, it was noted that when the law is expressed, whether orally or in writing, there is room for differences of opinion over the meaning of the language used. This has resulted in arguments about the meaning of particular words and phrases as well as how they are applied. Disputes over the meaning of the language of the law are part of legal argument and analysis. Eventually these disputes come before the courts to be settled and, in reading case law, you will uncover much that gives meaning and effect to legal language.

Although it is sometimes said that courts do not make law but the legislature does, judges play an active role in finding the meaning of legislation and applying it. In interpreting legislation, the courts are governed by statutory definitions, general rules and presumptions. These provide an interpretative framework that combines legislative requirements and judge-made conventions.

A good example of this combination of legislative interpretation and legal principle is demonstrated in the case of *Yuen Tam-wan*, which was first mentioned in Chapter 5. In this case, a husband had left his wife in China and moved in with the appellant, Yuen Tam-wan, until 1992. During this period a house was purchased, mainly using money provided by Yuen Tam-wan's mother, but it was jointly owned by the husband and Yuen Tam-wan. In 1988 the wife came to Hong Kong. In 1989 the husband gave his share in the house to Yuen Tam-wan in the form of a gift. This gift was challenged by the wife in the High Court in 1994 and the judge ruled that it was not lawful. This was because it fell within the meaning of *disposition* as set out in the Matrimonial Proceedings and Property Ordinance, s. 17 (1) (b), as its purpose was to avoid the claims of the wife for financial provision. In allowing Yuen Tam-wan's appeal against this decision, the Court of Appeal ruled that because there was no written agreement between the husband and Yuen Tam-wan regarding his share of the house, they needed to infer the intentions of the parties by reference to their conduct (a common law approach). By applying this principle, the Court determined that the husband only held his share of the house in trust for Yuen Tam-wan; therefore, when he disposed of this half share to Yuen Tam-wan by way of a gift, the Court held that this was not the type of disposition covered by section 17 (1) (b).

The obvious starting place for any interpretative task is the legislation itself. In Chapter 4 certain features of an ordinance were described, and by utilising these a court may initially find some guidance. Such structural aids to interpretation include:

(a) The long and short title which provide a description of the purposes and objects of an ordinance
(b) The preamble, which is a formal explanation of the enactment
(c) Headings, where the Ordinance is divided into sections or parts
(d) Schedules, which are designed to elaborate on particular details referred to in the ordinance
(e) Section headings, which contain catchword summaries of the section
(f) Interpretation sections, which provide definitions of key words and phrases

Apart from the definitions and interpretations in a particular ordinance and the structural aids referred to above, the Interpretation and General

Clauses Ordinance (Cap 1) also assists judges in this task. It is colloquially known as Cap 1 and a judge seeking to interpret a particular word or expression can refer to Cap 1 to determine if a definition already exists. Cap 1 contains definitions of many of the common and general words and terms that are used in ordinances, rules, regulations and by-laws. The word "person", for example, is said to include "any public body and any body of persons, corporate or incorporate, and this definition shall apply notwithstanding that the word 'person' occurs in a provision creating or relating to an offence or for the recovery of any fine or compensation". According to this definition, therefore, companies could be found guilty of certain crimes, such as manslaughter, which traditionally were thought only capable of being committed by individuals.

Other sources of assistance include:

(a) Dictionaries and other similar literary sources, *e.g.* thesaurus
(b) Previous court decisions (doctrine of precedent)
(c) Green and White Papers (see Chapter 4)
(d) Related ordinances (see for example the Dangerous Drugs Ordinance and the Pharmacy and Poisons Ordinance)
(e) *Hansard* reports and the *Government Gazette* (see Chapter 4 and below)
(f) International treaties and conventions (see for example the Bill of Rights Ordinance and the International Covenant on Civil and Political Rights)

Cap 1, s. 19 also provides that:

> "An Ordinance shall be deemed to be remedial and shall receive such fair and liberal construction and interpretation as will best ensure the attainment of the object of the Ordinance according to its true intent, meaning and spirit."

In understanding the role of the courts in interpreting legislative provisions, it must be remembered that the court's principal function is to give meaning to the law in accordance with the intentions of the legislature. Legislation takes precedence over common law and judges must apply the law so as to give effect to what the legislature wanted the legislation to achieve. Cap 1, s. 19 clearly reinforces this approach.

Rules of Interpretation

7.03 — This statement of policy is important and three rules have been developed by the courts to assist a judge in the process of interpretation.

These are the Mischief Rule, the Literal Rule and the Golden Rule. These approaches have, in varying degrees, been preferred by the courts at different times during the development of the common law. Cap 1, s. 19, however, appears to favour the Mischief Rule, but you should note that these approaches to interpretation act more like loose conventions rather than binding rules. They certainly do not have a precedent effect requiring that a court must apply one or the other, but they are principles of interpretation that a judge may use to justify a decision and produce what the judge believes to be the right result.

The Mischief Rule

7.04 — The classic definition of the Mischief Rule is to be found in a very old decision known as *Heydon's Case* (1584) 3 Co Rep 7a, 7b, but the general approach remains just as relevant today. Under the rule, judges are required to consider:

(a) What was the common law before the legislation?
(b) What was the defect or mischief for which the common law did not provide?
(c) What remedy did the legislature intend to provide?
(d) What was the reason for the remedy?

In this regard, the rule appears limited to situations where legislation has been enacted to cover a gap in the common law. It does, however, seek to determine the purpose of the legislation by identifying the "wrong" that the law was attempting to remedy and it is in these circumstances that the "rule" is most significant today. While the word "mischief" is difficult to define, it would appear that the "reason" why legislation was enacted is a reasonably safe definition of the term. It would appear relatively easy to find out what the law was before the ordinance came into effect, but this seems to limit the scope of the rule.

Some assistance in finding the reason for legislation can be obtained from reading what was said in the legislature (*Hansard*). In this sense, the court could simply read and follow the debate during the second reading of the bill. This use of the legislative proceedings is limited, however. In *R. v. Cheng Chung-Wai* [1980] HKLR 593 the Court of Appeal held that while a court could not generally refer to the proceedings of Legco to determine the meaning of an Ordinance, it could do so to determine the "mischief". In this case the court ruled that an admission, in the form of a police statement, that a person was a triad office bearer did not amount to claiming or professing under the Societies

Ordinance, s. 19. The court held that the mischief intended to be covered by the legislation was a claiming or professing so as to intimidate or gain some advantage. The reason behind this limitation on the courts' use of *Hansard* was based on the doctrine of separation of powers. If the courts were allowed to interpret freely what the legislature has said, they would be effectively putting themselves in the place of the legislature and thus interfering with the independence of the parliament. In the landmark decision of *Pepper v. Hart* [1993] 1 All E.R. 42, however, the House of Lords broadened the situations where reference could be made to *Hansard*. These include:

(a) Where legislation is ambiguous or obscure, or leads to an absurd result
(b) Where the material relied on consists of one or more statements by the promoter of the bill, together with such other material as is necessary to understand such statements and their effect
(c) Where the statements are clear.

The Literal Rule

7.05 — This is the most common approach to legislative interpretation and clearly the safest method for judges in that they simply apply what is said. This rule is based on the assumption that the intention of the legislature is to be found in the words used. The rule demands a literal reading of these words and not a determination of what the judge thinks might have been meant. In this regard, the judge will look at what is the primary or most obvious meaning of a word, drawing assistance for this from the sentence in which the word appears or even the legislation as a whole. The fact that in each case where a literal approach is adopted the circumstances will be unique, means that no one example can tell us how to apply this rule. Even so, the following case illustrates one example of its use.

In *Tam Ming-chu v. R.* MA No. 238/91 the accused appealed against the seizure and forfeiture of his boat because of its use in connection with unlawful gambling. In considering this appeal Bewley J. was required to determine if a boat fell within the definition of "other property" for the purposes of the Gambling Ordinance, s. 26, which states:

> "If in any proceedings under this Ordinance or otherwise on application by or on behalf of the Commissioner of Police, a court is satisfied that any money, gambling equipment or *other property*,

> not being immovable property, has been used in or for or in connexion with unlawful gambling or an unlawful lottery, the court shall order that it be forfeited to the Crown . . ." [emphasis added]

In dismissing the appeal, the judge held that if the main purpose of the boat at the time of its seizure was gambling then it was being used "in connexion with unlawful gambling" and, accordingly, was "other property" for the purposes of section 26.

The Golden Rule

7.06 — This rule has been called a gloss on or adaptation of the literal rule. It is said to be applicable where a literal definition of a word or phrase would give rise to an absurd situation. In such circumstances a court may look at the "purpose" of the legislation in order to apply the correct interpretation. Departure from the literal rule, however, is said to be restricted to situations where:

(a) There is a clear and gross anomaly
(b) The legislature could not have envisaged the anomaly and would not have accepted its presence
(c) The anomaly can be remedied without damage to the legislative intent
(d) The language of the legislation allows for such modification (*Stock v. Frank Jones (Tipton) Ltd* [1978] 1 All ER 948)

There appears to be little guidance, however, to help you determine whether such an anomaly exists. The following example demonstrates a possible application of the golden rule.

In *Re Application for Admission by a Barrister* [1981] HKLR 574, a member of the English Bar had come to Hong Kong on September 4, 1980 for the purposes of an inquiry, the original duration of which was approximately four to six weeks. Due to delays, the inquiry continued till June 1981. At this time the barrister applied for admission to the Hong Kong Bar. Section 27 (1) (e) of the Legal Practitioners Ordinance provides that a person applying for admission as a barrister must have been "ordinarily resident" in Hong Kong for a period of at least eight consecutive months prior to the date of application. In dismissing the application, the then acting Chief Justice, Sir Alan Huggins, ruled that while the applicant had been in Hong Kong for more that eight consecutive months the legislature intended something more than mere presence when it used the words "ordinarily resident". Intention and motive were factors to be considered and while his presence in Hong Kong had literally satisfied the time requirement, he was not ordinarily resident for the purposes of the ordinance.

As mentioned, the above rules are not actually binding nor are they distinct in the sense that they are to be chosen according to the particular circumstances. Judges will actually tend to adopt a unified approach to interpretation by combining the three rules. In this regard, a judge can:

(a) Give effect to the ordinary meaning of words or where appropriate the technical meaning of words in the general context of the legislation, determining the extent of general words also with reference to that context, and/or
(b) Consider whether the application of the words in their ordinary sense would produce an absurd result that could not reasonably have been the intention of the legislature and thereafter apply a secondary meaning, and/or
(c) Read in words that can be considered to be necessarily implied by the actual words of the statute and may even add, alter or ignore words in order to prevent a statute or part of a statute from becoming unintelligible, and/or
(d) Resort to certain aids of construction and presumption

Presumptions

7.07 — There are a number of presumptions that affect statutory interpretation and a court will presume certain things unless the legislation states otherwise. In *Lam Wan-kow and Yuen Chun-kong* [1992] 1 HKCLR 272, for example, the Court of Appeal held that because the Bill of Rights Ordinance did not indicate that it was retrospective, *i.e.* that it applied to matters before the passing of the ordinance, then the general presumption against retrospectivity should apply, *i.e.* that the provisions of the ordinance only relate to those matters that occur after it has been passed.

Other presumptions include the presumption against *strict liability*, the presumption against *the exclusion of natural justice* and the presumption against *intending inconvenience or unreasonableness*.

In summary, we can look at aids to statutory interpretation as being internal (the interpretations section, for example) or external (*Hansard*, for example) to an ordinance. Such aids are then applied, sometimes using one or more of the three "rules" of interpretation. It is arguable, however, that Cap 1, s. 19 states clearly what appears to be a preference for the Mischief Rule in that the courts must give such "fair and literal . . . interpretation as will best ensure the attainment of the object of the Ordinance". In addition, one or more of the above presumptions may be applicable.

Limitations on Statutory Interpretation

7.08 — Finally, it should also be noted that the power of the courts in Hong Kong regarding statutory interpretation is limited. As stated in Chapter 6, the jurisdiction of the SAR courts is limited in accordance with Article 19. In this regard, the earlier colonial principles have been retained and the courts can only interpret laws that have been passed by Legco. With the exception of the Basic Law, the courts have no jurisdiction, for example, over national laws relating to Hong Kong which have been passed by the NPC or its Standing Committee. Article 19 also states that the courts will have no jurisdiction over "acts of state such as defence and foreign affairs". Where such matters arise in the course of a case the courts must obtain a certificate from the Chief Executive that answers the questions of fact relating to whether this is an act of state and this certificate is then binding on the court.

While the SAR courts are empowered to interpret the Basic Law under Article 158, they are only authorised to do so within the limits of their jurisdiction. In this sense, they have no jurisdiction over those matters which relate to *acts of state*. In cases where the law concerns a matter that is the responsibility of the Central People's Government or that concerns the relationship between Hong Kong and the mainland the courts are required to seek an interpretation of the relevant provisions from the Standing Committee through the Court of Final Appeal. As stated in Article 158, however, the ultimate power of interpretation of the Basic Law is vested in the Standing Committee.

The Doctrine of Precedent

7.09 — In Chapter 4 we demonstrated how case law develops over time through the process of review by future courts. This process of review is governed by the doctrine of judicial precedent that holds that an inferior or lower court is bound by the decision of a previous superior or higher court. The general principle of precedent is that what was done before should be done again, like cases should be treated alike.

Judicial precedent requires that courts follow earlier decisions where the cases are similar in fact and law. The legal principle that governs this hierarchical system is called "*stare decisis*" which translates as "to stand by decisions". Under this principle, future courts at the same level (horizontal *stare decisis*) or at a lower level (vertical *stare decisis*) may be said to be bound to follow an earlier decision if the case is similar.

Vertical *stare decisis*

7.10 — In Chapter 5 the hierarchical system of the Hong Kong courts is described and it is this that gives the *stare decisis* principle its structure. The Court of Appeal is bound by decisions of the Court of Final Appeal, the Court of First Instance is bound by the Court of Appeal and so on. In the District Court and Magistrates Court, and where the Court of First Instance sits as the trial court, decisions are primarily based on an assessment of facts and evidence. Those courts are not often concerned with questions of refined legal analysis and accordingly do not set precedents. For Hong Kong this function is primarily carried out by the Court of Appeal and the Court of Final Appeal. The Court of First Instance, particularly in hearing appeals from the magistrates courts, however, may also create precedents.

At the vertical level the doctrine is quite strict. In other words, a lower court must follow the decision of a higher court where the case is similar in fact and law. A judge, however, may attempt to avoid having to follow a superior court's judgment by distinguishing it. This will be discussed in more detail later, but the easiest way of doing this is to distinguish the case on its facts. What lower courts cannot do is refuse to follow a higher court's decision by saying it was wrong. In the famous English case of *Broome v. Cassell* [1971] 2 All E.R. 187, Lord Denning M.R. convinced the rest of the Court of Appeal that the decision of the House of Lords (the most superior court in England) in *Rookes v. Barnard* [1964] A.C. 1129 was wrong. When *Broome v. Cassell* was appealed to the House of Lords, [1972] A.C. 1027, the court ruled that lower courts were obliged to accept the decisions of higher courts. The position in Hong Kong was clearly stated by Wong J. in *R v. Chan Sau-lin* [1994] 1 HKCLR 110 at p. 113: "The decisions of the Full Court, being the predecessor of the Court of Appeal, are binding on magistrates and any judge hearing appeals from magistrates." (p. 113)

All courts are, therefore, bound by all courts superior to them. In the case of *R. v. Yiu Lai-kuen* [1993] 1 HKCLR 215, for example, the Court of Appeal followed the Privy Council decision in *Attorney General v. Chan Nai-keung, Daniel* [1988] 1 HKLR 70 in deciding that an export quota was "property" for the purposes of the Theft Ordinance (Cap 210). Similarly, in *R. v. Lum Wai-ming* [1992] 2 HKCLR 221, Deputy High Court Judge Burrell followed the approach to Article 11 of the Bill of Rights Ordinance as set down by the Court of Appeal in *R. v. Sin Yau-ming* [1992] 1 HKCLR 127.

The Case of the Neighbours

7.11 — In Chapters 4 and 5, we looked at the case of two sets of neighbours, Mr Chan and Mr Cheung, and Mr Leung and Mr Lee. In Chapter 5, we found two cases, *Leeth & Co.*, and *Wayfoong Credit Ltd*, which appeared similar in fact to the circumstances of the neighbours. If we looked up these two cases we would have found that they were decided in the Court of Appeal. We also know that in both cases one neighbour had suffered $50,000 damage to his property. In accordance with the rules covering the commencement of civil actions, this would mean that both hearings, if they went to court, would be heard in the District Court. On this basis, there would be strong argument on behalf of Mr Cheung that the District Court was bound by *Leeth & Co.* and that Mr Chan was, therefore, liable for the damages to Mr Cheung's property. On the other hand, the court in *Wayfoong* ruled that the defendant company was not liable. On this basis, Mr Leung would argue that the court was *bound* by *Wayfoong* and that he was, therefore, not liable for the damage to Mr Lee's property.

Horizontal *stare decisis*

7.12 — Courts of equal status (horizontal level), however, usually do not bind each other, though judges prefer to follow decisions made at the same level of authority. This is of particular importance when considering the role of the Court of Appeal and Court of Final Appeal in the development of precedent. While the Court of Appeal does tend to follow its own earlier decisions, it is not strictly bound by them. It is, therefore, able to adopt a more flexible approach and respond to new needs as they occur. It will depart from previous decisions only after cautious consideration.

Hong Kong has adopted the English approach to this aspect of precedent and it affects both the Court of Appeal and Court of Final Appeal. In the English case of *Young v. Bristol Aeroplane Co. Ltd* [1944] K.B. 718, guidelines were laid down for how the English Court of Appeal (which is at the same level as the Hong Kong Court of Appeal) should deal with previous decisions. First, the Court of Appeal can choose between previous conflicting decisions. Over time the judges who sit on the Court of Appeal change and in some cases this has led to conflicting decisions. A future Court of Appeal when considering these decisions has the discretion to choose the one it thinks most appropriate. In *Attorney General v. Lau Chiu-tak* [1984] HKLR 23, the Court of Appeal seemed to go a step further, ruling that the court can reject all previous decisions and try a new solution. The Court of Appeal held that both previous decisions relevant to the case were wrong and that the Court of Appeal was only bound "to follow a single, clear previous decision of itself."

A previous Court of Appeal decision may also be subsequently overruled by a Court of Final Appeal decision. In such cases, the Hong Kong Court of Appeal would simply follow the Court of Final Appeal decision (see, for example, *Liu Po-shing* CA No. 520/84).

If a previous Court of Appeal decision can be shown to have been made in error due to ignorance of authority and/or faulty reasoning then it is said to be *per incuriam*, by carelessness. On this basis, the decision can be seen as *wrong* and a subsequent court is not bound by it. In *R. v. Shing Hing-sang* [1983] HKLR 1, for example, the Court of Appeal ruled that the decision in *R. v. Ng Chi-wah* [1978] HKLR 101, which held that there was a distinction between "professing" and "claiming" to be a triad was wrong.

Finally, while consistency and predictability are primary objectives, the Court of Appeal does exercise a considerable amount of flexibility in reaching its decisions. It would also appear that a greater degree of flexibility is to be allowed by the Court of Appeal in criminal cases than in civil cases. In this regard, the Hong Kong Court of Appeal has again followed the approach set out in *Young v. Bristol Aeroplane* stating that it should generally follow previous decisions on civil matters, but be more flexible in criminal appeals (*Ng Yuen-shiu v. Attorney General* [1981] HKLR 352).

Binding versus Persuasive Precedent

7.13 — Binding precedent occurs where a court is obliged to follow an earlier decision that is similar to the one currently being heard. In Chapter 3, it was noted that it was the *ratio decidendi* of the previous decision that binds the future court's decision. In many cases, however, courts will follow or apply the decisions and *ratios* of earlier courts not because they are obliged to do so but because they are persuaded that the legal principle in the earlier case is correct. The difference, however, between *binding* and *persuasive* precedent is unclear. By reading the case you can sometimes determine which is which, this being particularly true if the words "bound" or "binding" are used by the judges. In many cases, it is not so clear. The headnote of Hong Kong cases (in particular the Hong Kong Law Reports) is of assistance where certain words are used to describe how the court has treated particular cases. These words include: *applied, approved, considered, distinguished and overruled.*

> **Applied**—This describes situations where a court has determined that it is either bound by the previous decision or the legal principle of the earlier case is the correct one for use in answering the legal question that it is considering.
> **Approved**—This is used by higher courts when agreeing with the judicial reasoning of a lower court.
> **Considered**—This refers to the many residual (not applied or approved) cases that a court may refer to or be referred to during the course of the hearing. This does not mean that what the court says about these cases is not important. It may be extremely important as *obiter dicta*.
> **Distinguished**—A case is distinguished where a court does not wish to follow it. If it is a lower court it will have no power to overrule it, but even if it is a court at the same level the preferred approach is to distinguish the earlier case on the basis that the facts are different. This allows the court to say that because the facts are different then the legal principle of the earlier decision is not applicable. In *R. v. Leung Cheong* [1988] 1 HKLR 103, for example, the issue before the court was whether one act of prostitution and the passing of money to a third person would be enough to establish the offence of "living off the earnings of prostitution". The defence argued that the court should follow the decision in *R. v. Leung Chor* [1963] HKLR 825, where the court held that in the circumstances of that case the one act was not sufficient to prove the offence. In *Leung Cheong*, however, the court distinguished *Leung Chor* on the grounds that in that case there was no money paid to the accused whereas in *Leung Cheong* there was.
> **Overruled**—In some cases (see *Lau Chiu-tak* above), however, the courts are prepared to say that a previous decision at the same level or lower was wrong or that things have now changed and a new approach is needed. Then if the case is at a lower level, it can be overruled.

Being a common law jurisdiction, Hong Kong courts often make reference to other common law countries. In some cases, Hong Kong courts will follow these decisions. This is particularly true for English cases. But

R v. Cheung Wai-bun, Charles

Held:

1. **Whether the court was dealing with a common law abuse or an infringement of rights under the Bill of Rights, the factors to be considered (in particular) were: the length of the delay; the reasons for the delay; the conduct of the parties; prejudice to the defendant; and the public interest. (See p. 201, lines 24–30.)** *R. v. Norwich Crown Court, ex parte Belsham* **[1922] 1 WLR 54,** *Jago v. New South Wales* **(1989) 168 CLR 23,** *Barker v. Wingo* **407 US 514 (1972) considered.**
2. **As far as the length of delay was concerned, the court would take as a starting point the time at which an individual was officially advised that he was suspected of having committed a criminal offence. (On the facts this was August 1988.) However, as regards the general question of the fairness of a trial, the court would also take into consideration the length of time which had elapsed since the events occurred and the effect that lapse of the time might have (***e.g.*** the availability or capacity of witnesses) on the accused. (See p. 203, lines 3–9 and 25–30.)** *Foti v. Italy* **(1982) 5 EHRR 313 and** *Mills v. R.* **(1986) 26 CCC (3d) 481 considered.**
3. **Accordingly, the application was to be considered in the context of a 3 years and 9 months period (August 1988–May 1992) that the accused had to await a trial, in relation to events which had taken place some ten years earlier. (See p. 204, lines 5–7.)**
4. **The ultimate question (both at common law and under the Bill of Rights) was whether a continuation of the proceedings could be fair. It was for the accused to establish, on a balance of probabilities, that such proceedings could not be fair. However, where the delay was sufficiently excessive, as on the facts of the instant case, a presumption of prejudice arose; and it was then for the prosecution to rebut that presumption. (See p. 210, lines 11–20.)**
5. **Having regard to all the circumstances, including the public interest, the prosecution had failed to rebut the presumption of prejudice. The continuation of proceedings would amount to an abuse of process of the court. (See p. 212, lines 29–33 and p. 214, lines 9–12.)**

Application granted: stay ordered.

C. Nicholls, Q.C. and R. G. Turnbull, Senior Assistant Crown Prosecutor, for Crown.

G. Haldane, instructed by Haldane Midgley and Booth, for the accused.

Cases cited in the judgment:

Attorney General's Reference (No. 1 of 1990) [1992] QB 630, [1992] 3 WLR 9, [1992] 3 All ER 169
Barker v. Wingo (1972) 402 US 514
Bell v. D.P.P. [1985] AC 937
Connelly v. D.P.P. (1964) 48 Cr App R 183
Eckle v. Federal Republic of Germany (1982) 5 EARR 1
Foti and Others v. Italy (1982) 5 EHRR 313
Jago v. The District of New South Wales and Others (1989) 168 CLR 23
Kakis v. Government of the Republic of Cyprus [1978] 1 WLR 779, [1978] 2 All ER 634
Kemmanche v. France European Court 27.11.1991
Mills v. R. (1986) 26 CCC (3d) 481
Morin v. R. Canadian Supreme Court, in March 1992, Sepinka, J.
Mungroo v. R. [1991] 1 WLR 1351, 95 Cr App R 334
Neubeck v. The Federal Republic of Germany European Court, 12.12.1983
R. v. Askov (1990) 59 CCC (3d) 449
R. v. Bow Street Stipendiary Magistrate, ex parte Director of Public Prosecutions (1989) 91 Cr App R 283, (1992) 95 Cr App R 9
R. v. Derby Crown Court, ex parte Brooks (1984) 80 Cr App R 164
R. v. Kalanj and Pion (1989) 48 CCC (3rd) 459
R. v. Norwich Crown Court, ex parte Belsham [1992] 1 WLR 54
R. v. Sin Yau-ming [1992] 1 HKCLR 127
R. v. Telford, JJ., ex parte Badhan [1991] 2 QB 78, [1991] 2 WLR 866, [1991] 2 All ER 854, 93 Cr App R 171
R. v. William Hung [1992] 2 HKCLR 90
Rahey v. R. (1987) 33 CCC (3d) 289
Strunk v. United States 412 US 434 L Ed 2d 56
WKL v. R. (1991) 64 CCC (3d) 321

since 1 July 1997, no cases decided outside Hong Kong create binding precedents for the courts, even the House of Lords, whose decisions used to be binding (*R. v. Ng Kin-yee* [1994] 2 HKCLR 1). As mentioned in Chapter 4, the decisions of the House of Lords may continue to influence the Hong Kong courts, whether they relate to common law principles or legislation adopted by Hong Kong in the form of a copy of an English Act.

In other cases, the Hong Kong courts will also use and in some cases follow the decisions of other countries. In the extract from the headnote of *R. v. Cheung Wai-bun, Charles* [1993] 1 HKCLR 189 you can see that in some cases this may even extend to non-common law jurisdictions, *e.g.* the European Union (see pp. 94–5).

Whether precedent is binding or persuasive, it must be remembered that it affects both the interpretation of legislation and the determination of common law principles. As mentioned, the reasoning behind the doctrine is that consistency is important and, accordingly, if something was done correctly in the past it should be similarly done in the future.

EIGHT

THE LEGAL PROCESS

8.01 — In Chapter 2 the way the law is classified is discussed. One of these classifications observed a distinction between what is called substantive law, such as the law of tort or criminal law, and procedural law, *e.g.* the rules relevant to the bringing of an action to court, the trial process and the enforcement of the court's rulings.

Procedural law can in turn be divided into civil and criminal, that is, the legal processes and the rules that govern the bringing and hearing of a civil dispute or the commencement of a criminal prosecution and its trial. Such procedural rules must be followed and if they are not or there is a mistake in how they are applied then this may result in a court ruling that the matter start again or, in the most serious of breaches, that a court's decision cannot stand and must be overruled. Such a decision would be made by an appeal court (see Chapter 6). Many appeals are based on the contention that one side has breached a procedural rule or that the judge has made an error. In a criminal case, for example, the defence may contend that the confession of the accused was not given voluntarily. If this argument is successful then the confession may not be used as evidence. If, however, the trial judge allowed the confession to be used as evidence, the defence might appeal against the conviction of the accused on the grounds that this was an incorrect ruling and the exercise of the judge's discretion was inappropriate. This example also demonstrates another legal area that falls within the general classification of procedural law. This is the law of evidence.

The purpose of this chapter is to introduce the student to this large and complex area of law. It will begin by looking at the law affecting the prosecution of a criminal offence, then the procedure relating to the bringing and hearing of a civil dispute and the possible enforcement of the court's judgment. In the case of criminal and civil matters, the procedures for appeal, whereby a disatisfied party asks a higher court to determine whether or not a lower court or tribunal was right or wrong, are also discussed. Finally, the role played by the laws of evidence and the underlying legal principles for such rules are outlined.

Criminal Procedure

8.02 — Crimes come to the attention of the police in two main ways. The most common method is a report by members of the public, *e.g.* that their vehicle has been stolen or they were assaulted. In other cases, witnesses to a crime may report the matter to the police, for example that they saw someone climbing through an apartment window. Next, police detect crime themselves. This occurs where police observe the commission of a crime or perhaps after investigation determine that a crime has been committed and who the offenders are.

This is then followed by an arrest and a charge or, in less serious cases such as careless driving, the laying of an information and summons. Both events can initiate the trial process. The powers of the police to arrest and charge an offender, together with other associated matters such as seizure of property and the detention of the offender, are to be found in the Police Force Ordinance (Cap 232).

In Chapter 6 it was stated that criminal trials take place in the Magistrates' Court, the District Court or the Court of First Instance. The location of the trial is determined by the class or category of offence. There are three categories:

(a) **Indictable only.** The most serious crimes—such as murder, manslaughter, armed robbery, rape and drug trafficking involving large quantities of drugs—must be tried in the Court of First Instance before a judge and a jury. All these offences carry a maximum penalty of life imprisonment. The trial of these cases may be preceded by a committal hearing in the Magistrates Court where the basic facts (the case against the accused) are tested. The magistrate's task is to determine whether the matter should proceed to the Court of First Instance for trial. Unlike the trial, where the prosecution must prove the offence, the committal seeks to establish whether the prosecution has sufficient evidence on which to base its charge(s) and that if the matter goes to trial that there is the likelihood that the offender will be convicted. An accused, however, may elect to forgo full committal proceedings and, after certain documents have been put before the magistrate, the matter can begin immediately in the Court of First Instance. This is known as a "paper committal". After the committal the prosecution will draw up the indictment. This sets out the details of the crime charged as they relate to the elements of the offence.

(b) **Indictable or summary.** Some offences—such as theft, burglary, assaults and drug offences involving small quantities of drugs—may be tried upon an indictment or a summons (summarily). The decision as to whether the case will be heard by way of an indictment in the Court of First Instance, District Court or summarily in the Magistrates' Court is made at the discretion of the Secretary for Justice (previously known as the Attorney General), based on the seriousness of the offence and the likelihood of a substantial gaol sentence.

(c) **Summary only.** These offences—such as careless driving and illegal gambling—can only proceed by way of a summons and are tried in the Magistrates Court. The distinction between indictable and summary offences is best understood on the basis of the seriousness of the offence. The more serious crimes will be tried on indictment and the less serious (or minor) on a summons. Technically, the distinction refers to the legal documents (an indictment and a summons) that are used to commence the proceedings against the accused.

The Criminal Trial

8.03 — All offenders, regardless of the category of offence, will initially come before a magistrate. If the accused has been arrested and charged, he or she may be in police custody or on police bail. Bail is a conditional release mechanism that allows those who are charged with offences to be released so they can prepare their case, but on the condition that they attend the court at various stages of the proceedings and for trial. Bail may be granted by the courts or the police. In order to ensure this attendance, an accused may be required to deposit amounts of money with the court that will be forfeited if the accused fails to turn up at the trial, *e.g.* where the offender absconds. Other conditions, such as the surrender of travel documents, may also be imposed. The law relating to bail is set out in the Bail Ordinance. If the matter is commenced by way of summons, bail is unlikely to be relevant and the accused will have been notified of the date to attend the Magistrates Court.

Where the accused has been arrested and charged, an initial decision will be made as to whether the accused will be allowed bail or kept in custody. If the matter is to proceed by indictment in the Court of First Instance, the accused is likely to be kept in custody and future dates will be set down for the accused to appear before the magistrate once more. There could be several court appearances before a committal hearing takes place or the actual trial begins. During this time, numerous applications may be made by the defence and the prosecution. It can often take many months from when persons are first charged until they are actually tried in the Court of First Instance. This problem is exacerbated if a jury is needed (see Chapter 6).

If it is decided that the matter not be tried in the Court of First Instance but in the District Court, the procedures are much more straightforward. No committal hearing is required for a District Court case. First, a date is set for the first appearance by the accused in court. At this time, the accused is given the opportunity to plead guilty or not guilty. If the plea is guilty, the case proceeds on the basis of a statement of the facts. If these are not disputed and the facts disclose the offence charged, then the accused is found guilty and sentenced.

If the accused pleads not guilty then the matter must be listed (set down) for trial. Consideration is given to the length of the hearing (which often depends on the number of witnesses to be called by each side) and a suitable date fixed. Owing to the limited number of judges and, therefore, court time, it may be many months before the actual trial takes place.

If the matter is commenced by way of summons in the Magistrates Court, the accused is asked whether he or she pleads guilty or not guilty. If the plea is guilty the matter proceeds immediately to sentence. Once again, if the plea is not guilty, a date for trial must be fixed.

The Not Guilty Plea

8.04 — Excluding for the moment the role of the jury in the Court of First Instance, trials by way of a not guilty plea proceed in much the same way at all three judicial levels (Court of First Instance, District Court and Magistrates Court). This process can be shown diagrammatically (see p. 100).

As discussed in Chapter 6, the procedure is "adversarial". The prosecution or plaintiff (the accuser) must commence by stating a case. As we will discuss later, the accuser also bears the main responsibility of establishing the liability of the accused or defendant (the onus of proof) at a certain level (burden or standard of proof). If they cannot discharge this onus and burden, then the judgement must be for the accused or defendant. In a criminal trial this will result in the accused being found not guilty.

The trial procedure itself, as the diagram illustrates, involves the prosecution first presenting its case. In this regard, it will call witnesses, *e.g.* police officers, to testify under oath, or upon affirmation, as to what they

The Criminal Trial

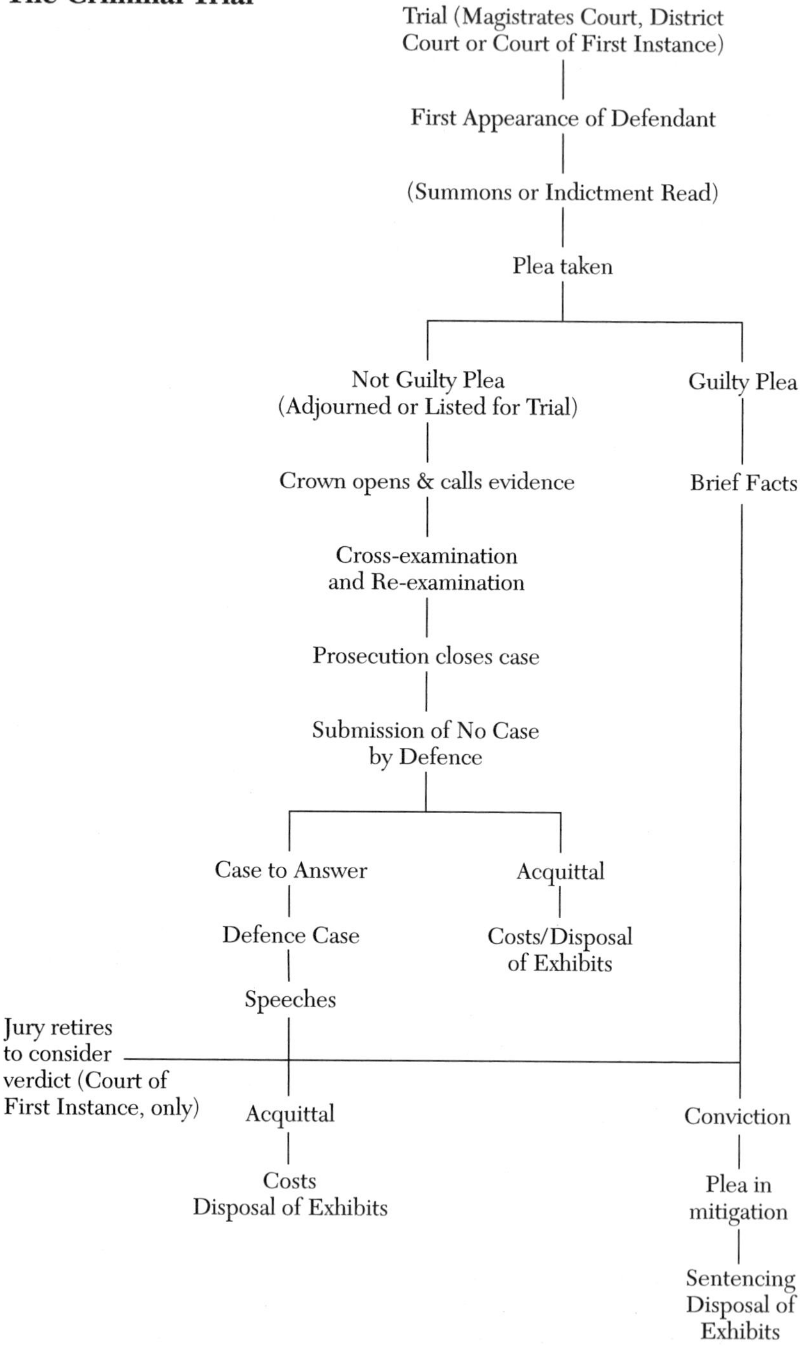

have seen, heard or done. The prosecution may also wish to introduce items, *e.g.* a gun or knife or documents. These are known as *exhibits*. Exhibits and the testimony of the witnesses form the evidence in the trial. As discussed later in this chapter, there are many legal rules that relate to such evidence and its presentation (admissibility) before the court.

Where witnesses are called by the prosecution, they will be asked questions (*examined*) by the prosecution counsel. During such examination, reference may also be made to other evidence, such as the gun or knife mentioned above. The prosecution's objective is to prove that something has happened, *e.g.* that the accused stabbed the victim, that he or she did so with a knife and that the knife now in the court room is that weapon. This is known as the examination in chief. After the prosecution finishes examining a witness, the defence has the right to cross-examine. The usual aim of the defence lawyer is to discredit the evidence or to raise a doubt as to the truth of what the prosecution witness has said. As will be discussed later, the defence may also seek to challenge the right of the prosecution to put certain evidence before the court or for the court to hear certain testimony from a witness. At the end of cross-examination, the prosecution may ask the witness some more questions. This is known as re-examination.

This process will continue until the prosecution's case is complete. At this stage, the defence can apply for the case to be stopped by claiming that the prosecution has not shown that the accused has a "case to answer". Later we discuss the prosecution's burden of proof, but the substance of this claim is that the prosecution has not been able to show that the accused is criminally liable, as set out in the particulars of the indictment or the summons.

If the judge or magistrate rejects the claim, the trial will proceed with the defence stating its case. Again, witnesses may be called to give testimony. Other evidence may be presented to the court. As with the prosecution case, there will be examination, cross-examination and re-examination of such witnesses. On completion, the prosecution, followed by the defence, will give their closing speeches.

At the end of the closing speeches by the prosecution and defence in the Court of First Instance, the judge will sum up the evidence for the jury, summarising the facts and highlighting those that are most important. Directions will then be given as to the points of law involved in this case, for example, the prosecution's burden of proof (to be discussed later) or what the jury may need to consider if a defence has been raised, *e.g.* provocation in a case of murder. The jury will then retire to a private room to consider its verdict. In all crimes, including murder, a majority verdict of five to two will be sufficient for a conviction. If the verdict is guilty, the matter is usually adjourned to a future date when the judge will hear argument from the defence that the accused deserves to be treated leniently (*mitigation*). Finally, the accused will be sentenced.

A similar procedure will be adopted in the District Court, except that it is a judge alone who will consider the question of guilt and thereafter the sentence to be applied.

Criminal Appeals

8.05 — As discussed in Chapter 6, there are limited rights of appeal for both defence and prosecution against conviction, acquittal and sentence. In general, the accused is allowed one appeal to a higher court. Further appeals are much more restricted and the accused must have very good reasons to be allowed to appeal for a second time.

Appeals from the Magistrates Court are heard in the Court of First Instance (usually by a single judge). In line with the principle of one appeal, the accused in these circumstances has an almost unlimited right to appeal against conviction and/or sentence. The prosecution may also appeal against any sentence it feels is too lenient. The Secretary for Justice also has a limited right to appeal against the acquittal of an accused. This is done by way of a "case stated" whereby the Secretary for Justice will request that a magistrate's decision involving a matter of significant legal importance be referred to the Court of First Instance or Court of Appeal. Strictly speaking, the Secretary of Justice does not appeal against a decision but seeks a review of the sentence or judgment.

Appeals from the District Court and the Court of First Instance are heard by the Court of Appeal. As with convictions and sentences handed down by the Magistrates Court, the accused in the District Court have almost unrestricted rights of appeal to the Court of Appeal. The Secretary for Justice may also appeal against a lenient sentence or again use the "case stated" option where it is believed that the accused has been wrongly acquitted. Depending on the type of appeal and importance of the legal principles involved, appeals from the District Court can be heard by a single Court of Appeal judge or a panel of three judges. In the case of a District Court appeal, or where an accused wishes to appeal against a decision of the Court of First Instance, permission (*leave to appeal*) must be sought and granted. Few problems exist where there is an appeal against sentence, but an appeal against a conviction must be based on a point of law, *e.g.* a misdirection of the jury as discussed in Chapter 6. The Court of Appeal will generally not hear appeals based simply on questions of fact, *e.g.* Was the accused present at the scene of the crime? In many cases, the application for leave will involve the Court of Appeal in an actual hearing and judgment. In these cases, the application for leave and the appeal itself are often combined. Appeals from the Court of First Instance are usually heard by a panel of three Court of Appeal justices. This panel must include either the President or Vice-President of the Court.

Finally, an accused dissatisfied with a Court of Appeal decision may seek leave to appeal to the Court of Final Appeal. This can only be against conviction (not sentence) and the application for leave to appeal must be based on an important point of law of sufficient legal significance for Hong Kong.

Civil Procedure

8.06 — This procedure covers an enormous variety of possible actions, ranging from, *e.g.* an action for monetary damages for breach of contract to actions relating to the legality of corporate takeovers and share issues. It also covers the procedures for judicial review in which a citizen, *e.g.* could be challenging the decision of a government department. As space does not allow for such coverage, and the objective here is simply to introduce the student to the basics of civil procedure, our discussion will be limited to an action for breach of contract.

As can be seen from the following diagram, however, even an action for simple breach of contract may be lengthy and complex.

Starting an Action

8.07 — All actions begin with the preparation of a writ by the plaintiff and its registration with the relevant court (District Court or Court of First Instance). It must then be served on the defendant with a section for the acknowledgement of service and an indication by the defendant of whether or not the claim is to be defended. Service involves the delivery by mail or in person of the writ to the defendant so that it can then be said that the defendant has notice of the claim. The writ is one of a number of legal documents which are called the *pleadings*. The general purpose of pleadings is for each party to provide the opposing side with certain detail and information concerning their case. This allows for each side to know what the case is against them prior to the actual hearing and, accordingly, to be able to prepare their case. Some other examples of pleadings are discussed below.

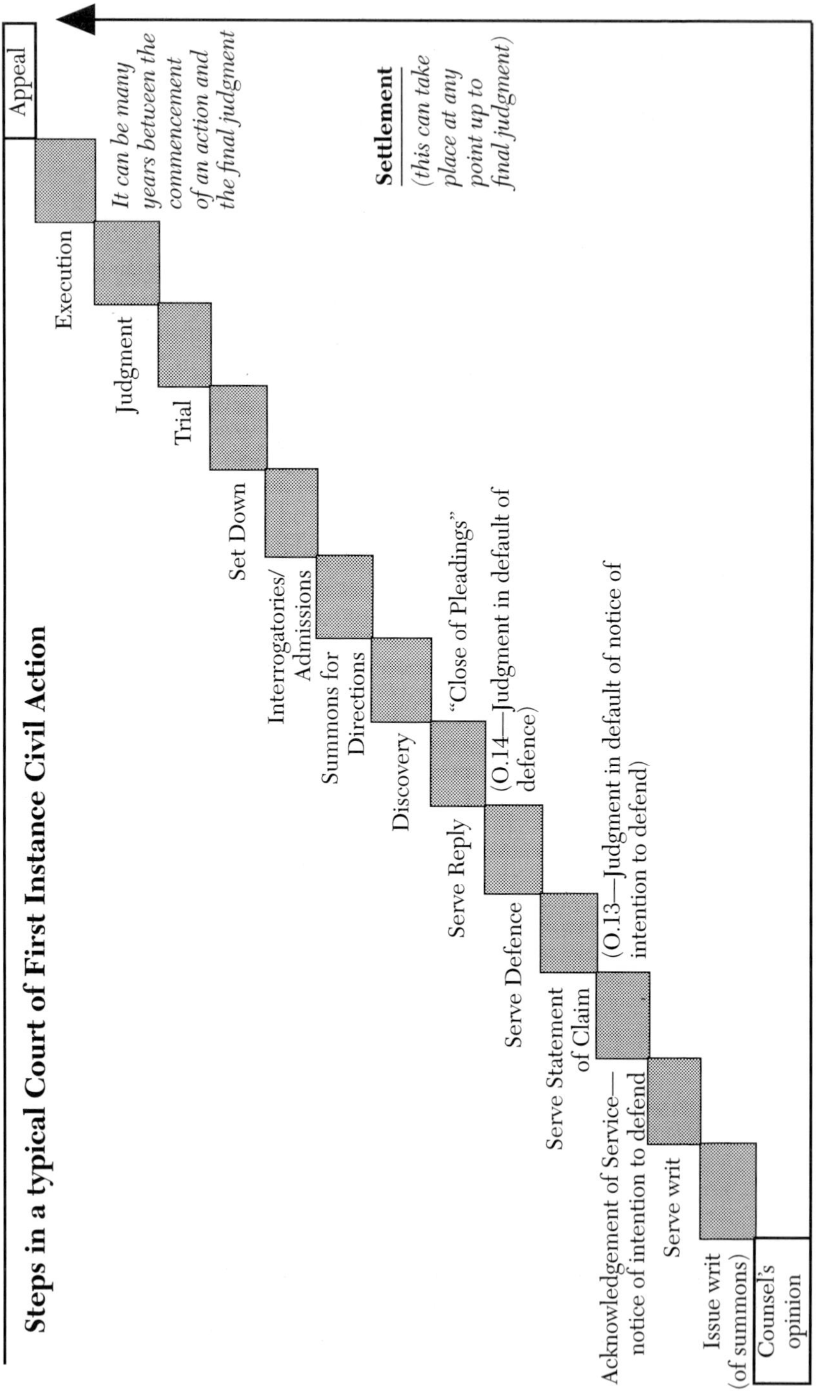

Steps in a typical Court of First Instance Civil Action

The writ must include either a brief or full statement of the claim. In the case of a breach of contract this includes the particulars of the contract, date, parties, conditions, price, etc. and the details of the claimed breach. It will also include the remedy sought. This may be for a fixed sum, such as the price or rent, or a claim for specific (*liquidated*) damages, general (*unliquidated*) damages and/or another remedy such as specific performance.

A defendant wishing to dispute the claim has 14 days in which to acknowledge service and file a Notice of Intention to Defend. A defendant may also have a claim against the plaintiff and set this out in a pleading called a Counterclaim. If no notice is filed, Summary Judgment will be entered against the defendant. The plaintiff may enforce the judgment in various ways, discussed later.

If the matter is defended, however, a number of other pleadings can take place. These can include a Reply to the Defence by the plaintiff as well as a Defence to the Counterclaim if one has been made. Quite commonly, both sides will ask for fuller and more precise information about each other's case. This is done through a Request for Further and Better Particulars. Many such requests can be made and where documents are involved in the dispute each side will seek to inspect them. This is known as *discovery* and each side is required to provide the other with a list of the documents they hold and to allow inspection. Failure to comply may result in an application being made to the court to order the other side to supply such particulars or allow access to documents. In some cases this may involve a hearing by the court and in large and complex cases there may be a number of these before the actual trial begins.

As stated above, the purpose of the pleadings is to provide each side with the details and information that go to make up claims, counterclaims and defences prior to the actual court hearing. In complicated cases where there is a lot of detail, many months (in some cases years) can pass between the original issuing of a writ and the hearing of the action.

The Civil Trial

8.08 — If the matter does proceed to trial, it will be heard in either the District Court or Court of First Instance, depending on the amount of the debt or damages claimed (see Chapter 6 on civil jurisdiction of the courts). In both courts the matter is heard by a single judge. The plaintiff will commence by stating the particulars of the claim and then present evidence in support. As with the prosecution's case in a criminal trial, this will be in the form of testimony from witnesses or the presentation before the court of evidence in the form of documents, such as written contracts or letters between the parties. In some cases the defence may object to the presentation of this evidence and before the trial can proceed the judge must decide such issues. A common practice in civil trials is for the exchange of witness statements and for this to stand as evidence in chief. Also, due to the exchange of pleadings, much of each side's evidence may be agreed, thus avoiding the need for it to be presented and cross-examined.

If evidence of a witness is not agreed, then once they have been examined by counsel for the plaintiff they can be cross-examined by the defence, the reverse being true when defence witnesses are called. On the completion of both sides' arguments there will be final addresses by each counsel. The judge will then retire to consider judgment.

Civil Appeals

8.09 — The appeal process in civil cases operates in much the same way as in criminal matters. In the case of a breach of contract, for example, the appeal may be against the judgment and/or the amount of damages awarded by the court. Once again, a person's rights to appeal are generally governed by the "one appeal" approach. Leave to appeal to the Court of Appeal, however, must still be sought and granted and appeals against the judgment must be based on questions of law rather than fact.

Enforcement of Judgments

8.10 — In our case of an action for breach of contract, let us suppose that the judgment is for the plaintiff in the amount of $100,000. In addition to this amount, the court will award costs to the plaintiff, which in some cases may exceed the judgment amount, particularly where barristers have been employed. This award of costs means that the defendant must pay some of the legal costs of the plaintiff. If the defendant had won then the reverse would occur. Both the judgment and the costs then become a debt. If the defendant does not pay, a number of enforcement options are available to the plaintiff. These include:

(a) **An execution order**—This empowers the court to seize the defendant's property, sell it at public auction and pass on the proceeds to the plaintiff.

(b) **A garnishee order**—Where the defendant earns a wage or a salary, an order can be made requiring that a proportion of this be paid periodically, *e.g.* monthly, in satisfaction of the judgment debt.

(c) **Bankruptcy**—A defendant who is an individual (not a company) can be declared bankrupt. This can result in all the individual's property being sold and all creditors, including judgment debtors, being paid from the proceeds.

(d) **Winding up**—If the defendant is a company, then the plaintiff can apply to the court to have the company wound up. The results are similar to bankruptcy for an individual and judgment debtors must take their place in line with all other creditors of the company.

Evidence and the Burden of Proof

8.11 — As stated previously, it is the accuser who bears the onus of proving the case against the accused. In criminal cases this involves the prosecution of an accused by the State, while in civil matters a plaintiff will seek some form of remedy against a defendant.

A case is proved where the State or a plaintiff puts forward sufficient evidence to discharge the burden of proof and, therefore, convince the court that the accused is guilty or a defendant is liable. The evidence of a fact is what proves it. Evidence can take many forms. In a case of murder, it could be the murder weapon, statements from a doctor on the cause of death, statements by witnesses who saw the killing and so on. In an action for a breach of contract, the evidence could be in the form of contractual documents, letters between the parties and oral testimony from witnesses. In any case, the duty of the court—either a judge or magistrate alone, or a jury—is to consider the evidence impartially and on the basis of this evidence alone reach a decision. As part of this decision making process, a judge or jury must also determine whether or not the prosecution or plaintiff has done enough to discharge the burden of proof.

The Burden of Proof

8.12 — This burden of proof can be divided into two types, a *legal burden* and an *evidential burden*. The legal burden determines who has the legal responsibility of convincing the court that it should accept their arguments and evidence in support rather than those of the other side. The evidential burden refers to the degree or extent of this burden. This differs for civil and criminal cases.

Criminal

8.13 — In criminal cases, the prosecution has the burden of providing (*adducing*) sufficient evidence to convince the court that the accused is guilty *beyond reasonable doubt*. This means that a judge or jury must be sure of the offender's guilt both in fact and in law. It is not required that there be no doubt at all but there be no reasonable doubt. Although there are some exceptions, *e.g.* the defence has the burden of proof if the defence of insanity is raised, the defence has no burden of proving its defence (*Woolmington v. DPP* [1935] A.C. 462). In practice, however, the defence lawyers will usually put some evidence before the court that is sufficient to raise a defence, *e.g.* provocation in a case of murder. If the prosecution discharges its evidential burden, the defendant risks conviction if he or she does not provide an explanation but, having done so, it is the prosecution who must disprove such a defence.

Civil

8.14 — In civil cases the onus of proof is also on the party bringing the action, the plaintiff. This onus, however, shifts in accordance with the relevant pleadings. Accordingly, a plaintiff will have the responsibility of convincing a court of the particulars of a statement of claim, but a defendant will also have the onus of supporting the statement of defence and, if applicable, any counterclaim. The civil standard or burden of proof is proof upon a balance of probabilities, or in other words that it is more likely than not.

The Rules of Evidence

8.15 — The requirement that evidence must prove the existence of a fact has led to the development of many rules that relate to whether the evidence is admissible; that is, can it be legally put before the court for its consideration? To begin with, only evidence that is relevant is admissible. While this sounds straightforward, in some cases it is not and legal argument may occur. This, together with other questions of admissibility, can result in a trial within a trial, known as a *voir dire*. Several of these could take place in any one trial, the end result in some cases being a considerable extension of the trial's length. The law of evidence consists of a number of general rules excluding evidence together with a series of exceptions to those rules. We have already mentioned one: that evidence should be relevant. Other rules concern improperly or illegally obtained evidence and evidence which is said to be secondhand (*hearsay*). In many cases concerning the admissibility of evidence, the judge has considerable discretion as to whether to allow or exclude it. The general guideline is that if it is relevant and important in establishing the truth it should be allowed. Many of the rules regarding the admissibility of evidence as well as the procedural requirements are contained in the Evidence Ordinance.

Due to the requirement in criminal cases that facts be proved beyond reasonable doubt, criminal cases best serve to illustrate the operation of some of these rules. In a criminal case, for example, police will often attempt to get a statement or confession from the accused. Any admission by the accused as to their role in an offence is extremely important evidence in any prosecution as it relieves the prosecution of much of its burden in proving the case. Where it is alleged, however, that a statement or confession was not "voluntarily" given, *e.g.* owing to torture or inducement, then the judge must decide whether it is admissible or inadmissible. If it is accepted that the statement was made involuntarily, then it will be inadmissible. On the other hand, items seized in a raid on a flat that are evidence of a crime, but where no search warrant has been obtained, will generally be admissible. As stated above, judges are given quite wide discretion to decide on the issue of admissibility, with the decision usually turning on a question of the *probative value* of the evidence, that is, the extent to which it will help establish the truth.

Secondhand or *hearsay* evidence is also generally excluded. This is because evidence should always be, where possible, *direct evidence* or proof of a fact. Statements by a witness that he had overheard a conversation is hearsay and generally inadmissible. What the courts want is to hear evidence from the persons who were actually involved in the conversation. One exception to this rule is known as "the dying declaration or confession". A person who hears a dying person's statement is allowed to tell the court what was said. In this sense, the court is prepared to admit the best evidence possible.

Even if evidence is admissible, however, we should also remember that it is subject to examination and cross-examination to test its credibility. What the rules of evidence attempt to resolve is the question of what is fair and just in the circumstances (without unfairly prejudicing any side in the case) and what is the truth.

The laws of procedure and evidence are not only large in number but are often complex and technical. Nevertheless, they form a vital category of law that not only serves to give order to the operations of the judicial system but also ensures that the system is fair and just.

NINE

THE LAWYERS

Lawyer's Jobs

9.01 — Lawyers do many kinds of job. Some spend all their time in their offices working for their clients, usually in partnership with other lawyers or as their employees. Some spend most of their time in court, as advocates. Some are judges or magistrates. Some work for the Government, some for businesses, such as banks or insurance companies. There are lawyers in the police and the army. Some are full-time teachers of law. Some of these jobs can be done by law graduates who have not completed their professional qualifications.

All those entitled to call themselves lawyers start off by entering one of the two branches of the legal profession and become either barristers or solicitors.

Entry into the Professions

9.02 — All entrants nowadays are graduates. They have obtained either a Bachelor of Laws (LL.B.) degree or they have a degree in some discipline other than law, but have done further studies in law at the degree level. In Hong Kong there are two law schools offering LL.B. programmes, Hong Kong University and City University of Hong Kong. Each course is three years long, after which one more year must be spent on practical training, which leads to the final qualification, the Postgraduate Certificate in Laws (PCLL). These and other entry requirements are covered by law, the Legal Practitioners Ordinance. This legislation provides the professional framework for the practice of law in Hong Kong. Other important aspects of this ordinance are dealt with later.

The new law graduate must then choose which profession to join. There are no other professional examinations, but for a solicitor two years of traineeship (previously known as articles) are required before professional admission, and two more years of practical experience before the new solicitor may set up practice or enter into partnership.

As soon as law graduates are awarded the PCLL, they may become barristers straight away (this is known as being called to the Bar). They cannot practise straight away, however, and must serve what is known as pupillage for one year. This is similar to the traineeship done by solicitors and, in both cases, the trainee solicitor or pupil works with a more experienced solicitor or barrister known as the master. This is an old and traditional approach to entering the profession that has changed significantly in other common law countries, *e.g.* Australia. The fact that it continues to be the practice in Hong Kong is a product of our colonial heritage and a reflection of the conservative nature of the legal profession itself.

It is also common for practitioners from other jurisdictions to seek admission in Hong Kong. Traditionally, Hong Kong's legal profession came predominantly from England, and English practitioners still enjoy special admission privileges. It is easier for them to gain admission than other lawyers from Commonwealth countries, such as Australia and New Zealand, and from the United States. These lawyers are deemed to be foreign lawyers and are required to undertake certain courses and examinations before being eligible for admission as a barrister or solicitor in Hong Kong. This does not mean that English or other foreign lawyers can be admitted very soon after they arrive in Hong Kong. The Legal Practitioners Ordinance requires that persons seeking admission have been ordinarily resident in Hong Kong for at least seven years prior to admission. Ordinarily resident, in these circumstances, is to be interpreted in accordance with the provisions of the Immigration Ordinance. No admission provisions have yet been made for lawyers from elsewhere in China. The extent to which, and for how long, the current requirements, restrictions and privileges will continue is unknown.

Barristers and Solicitors

9.03 — This distinction between barristers and solicitors still exists in Hong Kong but it has almost disappeared in other jurisdictions. It is peculiar to the common law of England, although most countries that have a common law tradition have now merged the two professions. In particular, the most populous common law countries, the United States and India, together with almost all the other former colonies, now see no need for separation. Many of the old differences between the two professions have also disappeared in England. Even in Hong Kong they are under threat and cannot be expected to survive much longer.

Where the professions have been joined (*fused*), however, lawyers still tend to specialise in what is known as advocacy. It is sometimes said that the solicitor is the law's equivalent to medicine's general practitioner, while the barrister is like a specialist. This is no longer a helpful analogy. Most barristers have very general practices, being happy to take any kind of well-paid work, particularly at the start of their careers. It usually takes a barrister quite a few years before it is possible to specialise and many never do. On the other hand, many solicitors nowadays are specialists. Many firms in Hong Kong are branches of international firms. There are some large local firms. Even in smaller firms, many lawyers work within a quite narrow speciality. In one sense barristers practise special skills. Though there are many solicitors who spend a good deal of time in advocacy, restricted to the lower courts or before tribunals or arbitrators, more barristers spend more of their time in court as advocates. At present, solicitors have no right of audience, that is they may not appear as advocates, in the higher courts.

The Future of the Professions

9.04 — In 1995, the Law Society, the professional organisation of solicitors, suggested that the two branches should be united but the Bar Association, which represents barristers, resisted the "marriage". The greatest privilege which the Bar retains is the right to appear as advocates in the Court of First Instance, the Court of Appeal and the Court of Final Appeal. Until 1996, solicitors were ineligible to be appointed as judges of the High Court (now Court of First Instance). This was altered to allow those solicitors with at least 10 years advocacy experience to be appointed to the High Court bench and the first, Mr Justice Peard, was appointed in 1996. As a colony, Hong Kong followed the colonial practice of allowing magistrates to be promoted to the District Court and from there to the High Court (now Court of First Instance) and even the Court of Appeal. In fact, the former Chief Justice, Sir T. L. Yang, followed that path. Interestingly, those who speak for the Bar continue to oppose changes to the rules that will allow solicitors the right to appear as advocates in the Court of First Instance, Court of Appeal or Court of Final Appeal.

Solicitors also have their privileges. Only they have the right to act directly for clients. As a general rule, barristers can only be brought in by a solicitor. In lawyers' language, the client must first seek assistance from a solicitor, who will then instruct the barrister.

Senior and Junior Counsel

9.05 — All solicitors are of the same rank but barristers are further divided into senior and junior counsel. However experienced or senior in years they may be, all barristers are called juniors unless they have been awarded the title of Senior Counsel. This is known as "taking silk", and prior to the changeover such barristers had the title of Queen's Counsel. Senior Counsel also charge more than juniors, as a rule. In the past, it was required that they be accompanied in court by a junior, whether there was work for the junior to do or not. While this is no longer the case, Senior Counsel are more often than not assisted by a junior. This is one reason why legal costs, especially those incurred during a trial, are so high.

High Court (Court of First Instance and Court of Appeal) judges are often appointed from the ranks of Senior Counsel, and Senior Counsel are also asked to act as deputy judges of the Court of First Instance. The qualifications necessary to become a judge or magistrate are discussed later.

Control of the Legal Profession

9.06 — One of the distinguishing characteristics of a profession is self-regulation. In Hong Kong, barristers are supervised by the Bar Association, while solicitors are subject to the control of the Law Society. The powers of both bodies arise from the Legal Practitioners Ordinance. These bodies are authorised to issue Practising Certificates and without one of these it is unlawful for anyone to practise as a barrister or solicitor. As discussed below, both bodies are also empowered to take disciplinary action against those who break the rules set down in the Legal Practitioners Ordinance. In some cases this may lead to a cancellation of someone's Practising Certificate.

Unlike other professions, however, both barristers and solicitors are also governed by the courts. They are admitted as barristers and solicitors of the High Court and their names are placed on court documents known as the Roll of Barristers and Roll of Solicitors. This is said to make them officers of the court and gives them certain duties and responsibilities. When appearing in court, all lawyers must respect the authority of the court. It is the judges, not the law, who insist on the fancy dress which barristers wear, as well as the black gown and distinctive white tie which solicitors also wear in the District Court. This costume is not required in the Magistrates Courts and it will be interesting to see how long the tradition prevails.

Both barristers and solicitors are subject to the judges' control, not only when appearing before them but in all stages of litigation. If they misbehave seriously enough, the judge may send them to prison until they apologise and promise not to continue or repeat their offensive conduct. This is called committing them for contempt of court.

It is not unusual for lawyers to commit criminal acts in the course of their work. The most common crime is stealing clients' money and scarcely a year goes by without some solicitor being struck off (see below). In some cases they have been sent to prison. In the past, lawyers in Hong Kong have been charged with huge bank frauds; with taking bribes in return for arranging for the Government to drop a prosecution; with providing a false passport and a gun to help another lawyer escape from justice; and with attempting to procure a schoolgirl for illegal sex. Some were barristers, some solicitors, some were in private practice, some worked for the Government.

In most of these cases, disciplinary action was first taken by either the Bar Association or Law Society. For solicitors this is done by the Solicitors Disciplinary Tribunal, and for barristers by the Barristers Disciplinary Tribunal Panel. Both bodies hold formal hearings and parties can be represented by other lawyers. The powers of both tribunals are similar and include the giving of warnings, suspensions from practice, fines and cancellation of rights to practise. The last of these is known as being "struck off the roll". In both cases, though, a barrister or solicitor is entitled to apply to the Court of Appeal for a review of the Tribunal's decisions.

In the legal profession, the requirement of ethical behaviour is stressed above all else. The distinguishing characteristic of all lawyers should be total honesty and a discriminating sense of what is legal and what is not. The future of the legal profession depends more fundamentally upon the public's confidence that lawyers are trustworthy than on their expertise. In the long run, clients may prefer other ways of organising their business and resolving their disputes if they find they cannot trust their own lawyers.

Secretary for Justice and Government Lawyers

9.07 — The Secretary for Justice (formerly the Attorney General) is the chief law officer of the Government and the administrative head of its legal offices. Even if a solicitor and not a barrister, the Secretary for Justice is also the head of the Bar (a collective term used for barristers). The Government's Legal Department was often referred to by lawyers as the Attorney General's Chambers, chambers being the name used for barristers' offices. Its departments deal with the Government's civil and criminal work. The Solicitor General heads the Policy and Administration Unit. The Director of Public Prosecutions (DPP) heads the Prosecutions Division. The State Solicitor is responsible for the Government's civil work, such as bringing or defending civil claims and drafting Government contracts. The Legislative Draftsman prepares legislation, including the translation into (or creation in) Chinese. The Law Reform Commission is chaired by the Secretary for Justice but has a Secretary responsible for its administration. The Director of Legal Aid has charge of the Legal Aid Department. The principal function of this Department is to deal with applications by the public for legal assistance for their cases, either criminal or civil. Such assistance may be in the form of an appointed lawyer or financial through the payment of part or all of a person's private lawyer's fees. Other Government departments also employ lawyers and there are lawyers in the various registries, such as the Companies Registry.

Judges and Magistrates

9.08 — Though the judicial service in Hong Kong is in the Common Law tradition and, therefore, based on that of England and Wales, there are many differences in Hong Kong. It has been a distinguishing mark of the judicial system in England that judges have been chosen from the practising barristers. This has not been the case to the same extent in Hong Kong. While many judges have been appointed from the ranks of Hong Kong's or England's barristers, this has never been sufficient for the numbers required. This was also true at the levels of the District and Magistrates Courts. Some young local lawyers did join the Government and then rise through the ranks from magistrate to the District Court to the High Court and the highest judicial offices. As mentioned, the previous Chief Justice followed this path. Many magistrates have come from England, but many others have been from Australia and New Zealand. While in recent years more local judges and magistrates have been appointed, it is likely that in the immediate future there will remain a number of foreign lawyers in both the judiciary and magistracy. They will include those who held these positions before the changeover but may also include new appointments. In some cases, notably the Chief Justice and Chief Judge, such positions can only be held by Chinese persons who are permanent residents of Hong Kong without the right of abode elsewhere (a foreign passport).

Magistrates

9.09 — Magistrates must have qualified as solicitors or barristers. They can have gained such qualifications in Hong Kong or the United Kingdom, Australia or New Zealand. They are governed by the Magistrates

Ordinance. Their initial appointment is for three years. Unless found unsatisfactory in some way, they are renewed. They may then be given a permanent appointment and serve until retirement age.

District Court

9.10 — District Court judges are usually appointed from the ranks of either private or Government lawyers, from the magistracy, or from abroad. They are appointed by the Chief Executive on the advice of the Judicial Officers Recommendation Commission. They must have five years experience in practice and are governed by the District Court Ordinance. They serve until retirement.

High Court

9.11 — The High Court is made up of the Court of First Instance and the Court of Appeal. Judges of the High Court are appointed by the Chief Executive and their appointments are governed by the High Court Ordinance. They are presided over by a Chief Judge. The normal qualification is 10 years experience as a barrister, District Court judge or Magistrate. As mentioned earlier, solicitors with 10 years experience as an advocate are now also eligible for appointment to the Court of First Instance. Government lawyers with similar qualifications are also eligible. Most current Court of Appeal judges have been drawn from the former High Court (now the Court of First Instance) but some have recently been appointed straight from practice. They are appointed by the Chief Executive on the advice of the Judicial Officers Recommendation Commission and serve until retirement. As mentioned above, the extent to which foreign judges will be recruited in the future remains unknown.

Court of Final Appeal

9.12 — The Court of Final Appeal Ordinance was enacted in 1995; but it did not come into effect until July 1, 1997. The Court is led by the Chief Justice, who, as mentioned above, must be Chinese and a permanent Hong Kong resident. The Chief Justice is appointed by the Chief Executive. The person can be a current judge, a retired judge, or a barrister with at least 10 years previous experience. There are the same eligibility requirements for a permanent judge of the Court. The composition of the Court for any particular case must include the Chief

Justice, three permanent judges and one non-permanent judge. Non-permanent judges are selected from a list of 30 and this includes other current Hong Kong judges, certain retired Hong Kong judges and invited judges from other common law jurisdictions.

In-house Lawyers

9.13 — Many large companies now employ lawyers. Banks, insurance companies, construction companies and firms of accountants may have lawyers employed full-time to advise them. They continue to use private firms of solicitors but see advantages in having their own internal legal advisers.

Other Careers

9.14 — Law graduates may decide not to enter one of the legal professions. Those who have completed their professional qualifications may prefer to take up other employment. There are lawyers who have given up the law for politics or business or who, having started as lawyers in the Civil Service, have switched to other branches.

The Law Teacher

9.15 — As in any scholarly discipline, there are a few lawyers who make it their life's work to prepare the next generation of practitioners. The concept of the law teacher or legal scholar, however, is not restricted to those employed full-time by universities. In the common law tradition, the judges have never given up the responsibility of scholarly writing and now there is a comfortable relationship of mutual respect between scholars, judges and other practitioners of the law, at least among the most able. It is not unusual to find the best textbook on a legal topic written by a judge or the best practitioners' book by a full-time law teacher. Moreover, some of the best scholarship, and some of the best writing, is to be found in the law reports. There are also many practitioners who teach part-time at Hong Kong's two law schools.

The Future

9.16 — With Hong Kong once again a part of China, it is likely that there will be freer interchange between the legal professions in the two jurisdictions. Already there are Hong Kong lawyers licensed to practise in China; others who are appointed to carry out notarial tasks in Hong Kong relating to matters in China; and there are lawyers from the People's Republic working in Hong Kong, though not yet practising Hong Kong law. There are moves to provide a rational set of requirements for foreign lawyers who wish to qualify for practice in Hong Kong.

One of the most positive indicators of Hong Kong's legal future is the rewarding co-operation that has for some years been developing between legal scholars in Hong Kong and the PRC. Already there is a substantial output of research and joint Master of Laws degree programmes at City University and People's University, Beijing. They augur well for the development of both the Hong Kong and the PRC legal systems that, different as they are, can be advanced by the strengthening of mutual understanding and the realisation that law must serve many of the same purposes in every decent society.

APPENDIX I

THE BASIC LAW OF THE HONG KONG SPECIAL ADMINISTRATIVE REGION OF THE PEOPLE'S REPUBLIC OF CHINA

Adopted at the Third Session of the Seventh National People's Congress on 4 April 1990

Preamble

Hong Kong has been part of the territory of China since ancient times; it was occupied by Britain after the Opium War in 1840. On 19 December 1984, the Chinese and British Governments signed the Joint Declaration on the Question of Hong Kong, affirming that the Government of the People's Republic of China will resume the exercise of sovereignty over Hong Kong with effect from 1 July 1997, thus fulfilling the long-cherished common aspiration of the Chinese people for the recovery of Hong Kong.

Upholding national unity and territorial integrity, maintaining the prosperity and stability of Hong Kong, and taking account of its history and realities, the People's Republic of China has decided that upon China's resumption of the exercise of sovereignty over Hong Kong, a Hong Kong Special Administrative Region will be established in accordance with the provisions of Article 31 of the Constitution of the People's Republic of China, and that under the principle of "one country, two systems", the socialist system and policies will not be practised in Hong Kong. The basic policies of the People's Republic of China regarding Hong Kong have been elaborated by the Chinese Government in the Sino-British Joint Declaration.

In accordance with the Constitution of the People's Republic of China, the National People's Congress hereby enacts the Basic Law of the Hong Kong Special Administrative Region of the People's Republic of China, prescribing the systems to be practised in the Hong Kong Special Administrative Region, in order to ensure the implementation of the basic policies of the People's Republic of China regarding Hong Kong.

CHAPTER I: GENERAL PRINCIPLES

Article 1

The Hong Kong Special Administrative Region is an inalienable part of the People's Republic of China.

Article 2
The National People's Congress authorizes the Hong Kong Special Administrative Region to exercise a high degree of autonomy and enjoy executive, legislative and independent judicial power, including that of final adjudication, in accordance with the provisions of this Law.

Article 3
The executive authorities and legislature of the Hong Kong Special Administrative Region shall be composed of permanent residents of Hong Kong in accordance with the relevant provisions of this Law.

Article 4
The Hong Kong Special Administrative Region shall safeguard the rights and freedoms of the residents of the Hong Kong Special Administrative Region and of other persons in the Region in accordance with law.

Article 5
The socialist system and policies shall not be practised in the Hong Kong Special Administrative Region, and the previous capitalist system and way of life shall remain unchanged for 50 years.

Article 6
The Hong Kong Special Administrative Region shall protect the right of private ownership of property in accordance with law.

Article 7
The land and natural resources within the Hong Kong Special Administrative Region shall be State property. The Government of the Hong Kong Special Administrative Region shall be responsible for their management, use and development and for their lease or grant to individuals, legal persons or organizations for use or development. The revenues derived therefrom shall be exclusively at the disposal of the government of the Region.

Article 8
The laws previously in force in Hong Kong, that is, the common law, rules of equity, ordinances, subordinate legislation and customary law shall be maintained, except for any that contravene this Law, and subject to any amendment by the legislature of the Hong Kong Special Administrative Region.

Article 9
In addition to the Chinese language, English may also be used as an official language by the executive authorities, legislature and judiciary of the Hong Kong Special Administrative Region.

Article 10
Apart from displaying the national flag and national emblem of the People's Republic of China, the Hong Kong Special Administrative Region may also use a regional flag and regional emblem.

The regional flag of the Hong Kong Special Administrative Region is a red flag with a bauhinia highlighted by five star-tipped stamens.

The regional emblem of the Hong Kong Special Administrative Region is a bauhinia in the centre highlighted by five star-tipped stamens and encircled by the words "Hong Kong Special Administrative Region of the People's Republic of China" in Chinese and "HONG KONG" in English.

Article 11

In accordance with Article 31 of the Constitution of the People's Republic of China, the systems and policies practised in the Hong Kong Special Administrative Region, including the social and economic systems, the system for safeguarding the fundamental rights and freedoms of its residents, the executive, legislative and judicial systems, and the relevant policies, shall be based on the provisions of this Law.

No law enacted by the legislature of the Hong Kong Special Administrative Region shall contravene this Law.

CHAPTER II: RELATIONSHIP BETWEEN THE CENTRAL AUTHORITIES AND THE HONG KONG SPECIAL ADMINISTRATIVE REGION

Article 12

The Hong Kong Special Administrative Region shall be a local administrative region of the People's Republic of China, which shall enjoy a high degree of autonomy and come directly under the Central People's Government.

Article 13

The Central People's Government shall be responsible for the foreign affairs relating to the Hong Kong Special Administrative Region.

The Ministry of Foreign Affairs of the People's Republic of China shall establish an office in Hong Kong to deal with foreign affairs.

The Central People's Government authorizes the Hong Kong Special Administrative Region to conduct relevant external affairs on its own in accordance with this Law.

Article 14

The Central People's Government shall be responsible for the defence of the Hong Kong Special Administrative Region.

The Government of the Hong Kong Special Administrative Region shall be responsible for the maintenance of public order in the Region.

Military forces stationed by the Central People's Government in the Hong Kong Special Administrative Region for defence shall not interfere in the local affairs of the Region. The Government of the Hong Kong Special Administrative Region may, when necessary, ask the Central People's Government for assistance from the garrison in the maintenance of public order and in disaster relief.

In addition to abiding by national laws, members of the garrison shall abide by the laws of the Hong Kong Special Administrative Region.

Expenditure for the garrison shall be borne by the Central People's Government.

Article 15

The Central People's Government shall appoint the Chief Executive and the principal officials of the executive authorities of the Hong Kong Special Administrative Region in accordance with the provisions of Chapter IV of this Law.

Article 16

The Hong Kong Special Administrative Region shall be vested with executive power. It shall, on its own, conduct the administrative affairs of the Region in accordance with the relevant provisions of this Law.

Article 17

The Hong Kong Special Administrative Region shall be vested with legislative power.

Laws enacted by the legislature of the Hong Kong Special Administrative Region must be reported to the Standing Committee of the National People's Congress for the record. The reporting for record shall not affect the entry into force of such laws.

If the Standing Committee of the National People's Congress, after consulting the Committee for the Basic Law of the Hong Kong Special Administrative Region under it, considers that any law enacted by the legislature of the Region is not in conformity with the provisions of this Law regarding affairs within the responsibility of the Central Authorities or regarding the relationship between the Central Authorities and the Region, the Standing Committee may return the law in question but shall not amend it. Any law returned by the Standing Committee of the National People's Congress shall immediately be invalidated. This invalidation shall not have retroactive effect, unless otherwise provided for in the laws of the Region.

Article 18

The laws in force in the Hong Kong Special Administrative Region shall be this Law, the laws previously in force in Hong Kong as provided for in Article 8 of this Law, and the laws enacted by the legislature of the Region.

National laws shall not be applied in the Hong Kong Special Administrative Region except for those listed in Annex III to this Law. The laws listed therein shall be applied locally by way of promulgation or legislation by the Region.

The Standing Committee of the National People's Congress may add to or delete from the list of laws in Annex III after consulting its Committee for the Basic Law of the Hong Kong Special Administrative Region and the government of the Region. Laws listed in Annex III to this Law shall be confined to those relating to defence and foreign affairs as well as other matters outside the limits of the autonomy of the Region as specified by this Law.

In the event that the Standing Committee of the National People's Congress decides to declare a state of war or, by reason of turmoil within the Hong Kong Special Administrative Region which endangers national unity or security and is beyond the control of the government of the Region, decides that the Region is in a state of emergency, the Central People's Government may issue and order applying the relevant national laws in the Region.

Article 19

The Hong Kong Special Administrative Region shall be vested with independent judicial power, including that of final adjudication.

The courts of the Hong Kong Special Administrative Region shall have jurisdiction over all cases in the Region, except that the restrictions on their jurisdiction imposed by the legal system and principles previously in force in Hong Kong shall be maintained.

The courts of the Hong Kong Special Administrative Region shall have no jurisdiction over acts of state such as defence and foreign affairs. The courts of the Region shall obtain a certificate from the Chief Executive on questions of fact concerning acts of state such as defence and foreign affairs whenever such questions arise in the adjudication of cases. This certificate shall be binding on the courts. Before issuing such a certificate, the Chief Executive shall obtain a certifying document from the Central People's Government.

Article 20

The Hong Kong Special Administrative Region may enjoy other powers granted to it by the National People's Congress, the Standing Committee of the National People's Congress or the Central People's Government.

Article 21

Chinese citizens who are residents of the Hong Kong Special Administrative Region shall be entitled to participate in the management of state affairs according to law. In accordance with the assigned number of seats and the selection method specified by the National People's Congress, the Chinese citizens among the residents of the Hong Kong Special Administrative Region shall locally elect deputies of the Region to the National People's Congress to participate in the work of the highest organ of state power.

Article 22

No department of the Central People's Government and no province, autonomous region, or municipality directly under the Central Government may interfere in the affairs which the Hong Kong Special Administrative Region administers on its own in accordance with this Law.

If there is a need for departments of the Central Government, or for provinces, autonomous regions, or municipalities directly under the Central Government to set up offices in the Hong Kong Special Administrative Region, they must obtain the consent of the government of the Region and the approval of the Central People's Government.

All offices set up in the Hong Kong Special Administrative Region by departments of the Central Government, or by provinces, autonomous regions, or municipalities directly under the Central Government, and the personnel of these offices shall abide by the laws of the Region.

For entry into the Hong Kong Special Administrative Region, people from other parts of China must apply for approval. Among them, the number of persons who enter the Region for the purpose of settlement shall be determined by the competent authorities of the Central People's Government after consulting the government of the Region.

The Hong Kong Special Administrative Region may establish an office in Beijing.

Article 23

The Hong Kong Special Administrative Region shall enact laws on its own to prohibit any act of treason, secession, sedition, subversion against the Central People's Government, or theft of state secrets, to prohibit foreign political organizations or bodies from conducting political activities in the Region, and to prohibit political organizations or bodies of the Region from establishing ties with foreign political organizations or bodies.

CHAPTER III: FUNDAMENTAL RIGHTS AND DUTIES OF THE RESIDENTS

Article 24

Residents of the Hong Kong Special Administrative Region ("Hong Kong residents") shall include permanent residents and non-permanent residents.

The permanent residents of the Hong Kong Special Administrative Region shall be:

(1) Chinese citizens born in Hong Kong before or after the establishment of the Hong Kong Special Administrative Region;
(2) Chinese citizens who have ordinarily resided in Hong Kong for a continuous period of not less than seven years before or after the establishment of the Hong Kong Special Administrative Region;
(3) Persons of Chinese nationality born outside Hong Kong of those residents listed in categories (1) and (2);
(4) Persons not of Chinese nationality who have entered Hong Kong with valid travel documents, have ordinarily resided in Hong Kong for a continuous period of not less than seven years and have taken Hong Kong as their place of permanent residence before or after the establishment of the Hong Kong Special Administrative Region;
(5) Persons under 21 years of age born in Hong Kong of those residents listed in category (4) before or after the establishment of the Hong Kong Special Administrative Region; and
(6) Persons other than those residents listed in categories (1) to (5), who, before the establishment of the Hong Kong Special Administrative Region, had the right of abode in Hong Kong only.

The above-mentioned residents shall have the right of abode in the Hong Kong Special Administrative Region and shall be qualified to obtain, in accordance with the laws of the Region, permanent identity cards which state their right of abode.

The non-permanent residents of the Hong Kong Special Administrative Region shall be persons who are qualified to obtain Hong Kong identity cards in accordance with the laws of the Region but have no right of abode.

Article 25

All Hong Kong residents shall be equal before the law.

Article 26

Permanent residents of the Hong Kong Special Administrative Region shall have the right to vote and the right to stand for election in accordance with law.

Article 27

Hong Kong residents shall have freedom of speech, of the press and of publication; freedom of association, of assembly, of procession and of demonstration; and the right and freedom to form and join trade unions, and to strike.

Article 28

The freedom of the person of Hong Kong residents shall be inviolable.

No Hong Kong resident shall be subjected to arbitrary or unlawful arrest, detention or imprisonment. Arbitrary or unlawful search of the body of any resident or deprivation or restriction of the freedom of the person shall be prohibited. Torture of any resident or arbitrary or unlawful deprivation of the life of any resident shall be prohibited.

Article 29
The homes and other premises of Hong Kong residents shall be inviolable. Arbitrary or unlawful search of, or intrusion into, a resident's home or other premises shall be prohibited.

Article 30
The freedom and privacy of communication of Hong Kong residents shall be protected by law. No department or individual may, on any grounds, infringe upon the freedom and privacy of communication of residents except that the relevant authorities may inspect communication in accordance with legal procedures to meet the needs of public security or of investigation into criminal offences.

Article 31
Hong Kong residents shall have freedom of movement within the Hong Kong Special Administrative Region and freedom of emigration to other countries and regions. They shall have freedom to travel and to enter or leave the Region. Unless restrained by law, holders of valid travel documents shall be free to leave the Region without special authorization.

Article 32
Hong Kong residents shall have freedom of conscience.

Hong Kong residents shall have freedom of religious belief and freedom to preach and to conduct and participate in religious activities in public.

Article 33
Hong Kong residents shall have freedom of choice of occupation.

Article 34
Hong Kong residents shall have freedom to engage in academic research, literary and artistic creation, and other cultural activities.

Article 35
Hong Kong residents shall have the right to confidential legal advice, access to the courts, choice of lawyers for timely protection of their lawful rights and interests or for representation in the courts, and to judicial remedies.

Hong Kong residents shall have the right to institute legal proceedings in the courts against the acts of the executive authorities and their personnel.

Article 36
Hong Kong residents shall have the right to social welfare in accordance with law. The welfare benefits and retirement security of the labour force shall be protected by law.

Article 37
The freedom of marriage of Hong Kong residents and their right to raise a family freely shall be protected by law.

Article 38
Hong Kong residents shall enjoy the other rights and freedoms safeguarded by the laws of the Hong Kong Special Administrative Region.

Article 39
The provisions of the International Covenant on Civil and Political Rights, the International Covenant on Economic, Social and Cultural Rights, and international labour conventions as applied to Hong Kong shall remain in force and shall be implemented through the laws of the Hong Kong Special Administrative Region.

The rights and freedoms enjoyed by Hong Kong residents shall not be restricted unless as prescribed by law. Such restrictions shall not contravene the provisions of the preceding paragraph of this Article.

Article 40
The lawful traditional rights and interests of the indigenous inhabitants of the "New Territories" shall be protected by the Hong Kong Special Administrative Region.

Article 41
Persons in the Hong Kong Special Administrative Region other than Hong Kong residents shall, in accordance with law, enjoy the rights and freedoms of Hong Kong residents prescribed in this Chapter.

Article 42
Hong Kong residents and other persons in Hong Kong shall have the obligation to abide by the laws in force in the Hong Kong Special Administrative Region.

CHAPTER IV: POLITICAL STRUCTURE

Section 1: The Chief Executive

Article 43
The Chief Executive of the Hong Kong Special Administrative Region shall be the head of the Hong Kong Special Administrative Region and shall represent the Region.

The Chief Executive of the Hong Kong Special Administrative Region shall be accountable to the Central People's Government and the Hong Kong Special Administrative Region in accordance with the provisions of this Law.

Article 44
The Chief Executive of the Hong Kong Special Administrative Region shall be a Chinese citizen of not less than 40 years of age who is a permanent resident of the Region with no right of abode in any foreign country and has ordinarily resided in Hong Kong for a continuous period of not less than 20 years.

Article 45

The Chief Executive of the Hong Kong Special Administrative Region shall be selected by election or through consultations held locally and be appointed by the Central People's Government.

The method for selecting the Chief Executive shall be specified in the light of the actual situation in the Hong Kong Special Administrative Region and in accordance with the principle of gradual and orderly progress. The ultimate aim is the selection of the Chief Executive by universal suffrage upon nomination by a broadly representative nominating committee in accordance with democratic procedures.

The specific method for selecting the Chief Executive is prescribed in Annex I: "Method for the Selection of the Chief Executive of the Hong Kong Special Administrative Region".

Article 46

The term of office of the Chief Executive of the Hong Kong Special Administrative Region shall be five years. He or she may serve for not more than two consecutive terms.

Article 47

The Chief Executive of the Hong Kong Special Administrative Region must be a person of integrity, dedicated to his or her duties.

The Chief Executive, on assuming office, shall declare his or her assets to the Chief Justice of the Court of Final Appeal of the Hong Kong Special Administrative Region. This declaration shall be put on record.

Article 48

The Chief Executive of the Hong Kong Special Administrative Region shall exercise the following powers and functions:

(1) To lead the government of the Region;

(2) To be responsible for the implementation of this Law and other laws which, in accordance with this Law, apply in the Hong Kong Special Administrative Region;

(3) To sign bills passed by the Legislative Council and to promulgate laws; To sign budgets passed by the Legislative Council and report the budgets and final accounts to the Central People's Government for the record;

(4) To decide on government policies and to issue executive orders;

(5) To nominate and to report to the Central People's Government for appointment the following principal officials: Secretaries and Deputy Secretaries of Departments, Directors of Bureaux, Commissioner Against Corruption, Director of Audit, Commissioner of Police, Director of Immigration and Commissioner of Customs and Excise; and to recommend to the Central People's Government the removal of the above-mentioned officials;

(6) To appoint or remove judges of the courts at all levels in accordance with legal procedures;

(7) To appoint or remove holders of public office in accordance with legal procedures;

(8) To implement the directives issued by the Central People's Government in respect of the relevant matters provided for in this Law;
(9) To conduct, on behalf of the Government of the Hong Kong Special Administrative Region, external affairs and other affairs as authorized by the Central Authorities;
(10) To approve the introduction of motions regarding revenues or expenditure to the Legislative Council;
(11) To decide, in the light of security and vital public interests, whether government officials or other personnel in charge of government affairs should testify or give evidence before the Legislative Council or its committees;
(12) To pardon persons convicted of criminal offences or commute their penalties; and
(13) To handle petitions and complaints.

Article 49
If the Chief Executive of the Hong Kong Special Administrative Region considers that a bill passed by the Legislative Council is not compatible with the overall interests of the Region, he or she may return it to the Legislative Council within three months for reconsideration. If the Legislative Council passes the original bill again by not less than a two-thirds majority of all the members, the Chief Executive must sign and promulgate it within one month, or act in accordance with the provisions of Article 50 of this Law.

Article 50
If the Chief Executive of the Hong Kong Special Administrative Region refuses to sign a bill passed the second time by the Legislative Council, or the Legislative Council refuses to pass a budget or any other important bill introduced by the government, and if consensus still cannot be reached after consultations, the Chief Executive may dissolve the Legislative Council.

The Chief Executive must consult the Executive Council before dissolving the Legislative Council. The Chief Executive may dissolve the Legislative Council only once in each term of his or her office.

Article 51
If the Legislative Council of the Hong Kong Special Administrative Region refuses to pass the budget introduced by the government, the Chief Executive may apply to the Legislative Council for provisional appropriations. If appropriation of public funds cannot be approved because the Legislative Council has already been dissolved, the Chief Executive may, prior to the election of the new Legislative Council, approve provisional short-term appropriations according to the level of expenditure of the previous fiscal year.

Article 52
The Chief Executive of the Hong Kong Special Administrative Region must resign under any of the following circumstances:

(1) When he or she loses the ability to discharge his or her duties as a result of serious illness or other reasons;
(2) When, after the Legislative Council is dissolved because he or she twice refuses to sign a bill passed by it, the new Legislative Council

again passes by a two-thirds majority of all the members the original bill in dispute, but he or she still refuses to sign it; and

(3) When, after the Legislative Council is dissolved because it refuses to pass a budget or any other important bill, the new Legislative Council still refuses to pass the original bill in dispute.

Article 53

If the Chief Executive of the Hong Kong Special Administrative Region is not able to discharge his or her duties for a short period, such duties shall temporarily be assumed by the Administrative Secretary, Financial Secretary or Secretary of Justice in this order of precedence.

In the event that the office of Chief Executive becomes vacant, a new Chief Executive shall be selected within six months in accordance with the provisions of Article 45 of this Law. During the period of vacancy, his or her duties shall be assumed according to the provisions of the preceding paragraph.

Article 54

The Executive Council of the Hong Kong Special Administrative Region shall be an organ for assisting the Chief Executive in policy-making.

Article 55

Members of the Executive Council of the Hong Kong Special Administrative Region shall be appointed by the Chief Executive from among the principal officials of the executive authorities, members of the Legislative Council and public figures. Their appointment or removal shall be decided by the Chief Executive. The term of office of members of the Executive Council shall not extend beyond the expiry of the term of office of the Chief Executive who appoints them.

Members of the Executive Council of the Hong Kong Special Administrative Region shall be Chinese citizens who are permanent residents of the Region with no right of abode in any foreign country.

The Chief Executive may, as he or she deems necessary, invite other persons concerned to sit in on meetings of the Council.

Article 56

The Executive Council of the Hong Kong Special Administrative Region shall be presided over by the Chief Executive.

Except for the appointment, removal and disciplining of officials and the adoption of measures in emergencies, the Chief Executive shall consult the Executive Council before making important policy decisions, introducing bills to the Legislative Council, making subordinate legislation, or dissolving the Legislative Council.

If the Chief Executive does not accept a majority opinion of the Executive Council, he or she shall put the specific reasons on record.

Article 57

A Commission Against Corruption shall be established in the Hong Kong Special Administrative Region. It shall function independently and be accountable to be Chief Executive.

Article 58

A Commission of Audit shall be established in the Hong Kong Special Administrative Region. It shall function independently and be accountable to the Chief Executive.

Section 2: The Executive Authorities

Article 59

The Government of the Hong Kong Special Administrative Region shall be the executive authorities of the Region.

Article 60

The head of the Government of the Hong Kong Special Administrative Region shall be the Chief Executive of the Region.

A Department of Administration, a Department of Finance, a Department of Justice, and various bureaux, divisions and commissions shall be established in the Government of the Hong Kong Special Administrative Region.

Article 61

The principal officials of the Hong Kong Special Administrative Region shall be Chinese citizens who are permanent residents of the Region with no right of abode in any foreign country and have ordinarily resided in Hong Kong for a continuous period of not less than 15 years.

Article 62

The Government of the Hong Kong Special Administrative Region shall exercise the following powers and functions:

(1) To formulate and implement policies;
(2) To conduct administrative affairs;
(3) To conduct external affairs as authorized by the Central People's Government under this Law;
(4) To draw up and introduce budgets and final accounts;
(5) To draft and introduce bills, motions and subordinate legislation; and
(6) To designate officials to sit in on the meetings of the Legislative Council and to speak on behalf of the government.

Article 63

The Department of Justice of the Hong Kong Special Administrative Region shall control criminal prosecutions, free from any interference.

Article 64

The Government of the Hong Kong Special Administrative Region must abide by the law and be accountable to the Legislative Council of the Region: it shall implement laws passed by the Council and already in force; it shall present regular policy addresses to the Council; it shall answer questions raised by members of the Council; and it shall obtain approval from the Council for taxation and public expenditure.

Article 65
The previous system of establishing advisory bodies by the executive authorities shall be maintained.

Section 3: The Legislature

Article 66
The Legislative Council of the Hong Kong Special Administrative Region shall be the legislature of the Region.

Article 67
The Legislative Council of the Hong Kong Special Administrative Region shall be composed of Chinese citizens who are permanent residents of the Region with no right of abode in any foreign country. However, permanent residents of the Region who are not of Chinese nationality or who have the right of abode in foreign countries may also be elected members of the Legislative Council of the Region, provided that the proportion of such members does not exceed 20 percent of the total membership of the Council.

Article 68
The Legislative Council of the Hong Kong Special Administrative Region shall be constituted by election.

The method for forming the Legislative Council shall be specified in the light of the actual situation in the Hong Kong Special Administrative Region and in accordance with the principle of gradual and orderly progress. The ultimate aim is the election of all the members of the Legislative Council by universal suffrage.

The specific method for forming the Legislative Council and its procedures for voting on bills and motions are prescribed in Annex II: "Method for the Formation of the Legislative Council of the Hong Kong Special Administrative Region and Its Voting Procedures".

Article 69
The term of office of the Legislative Council of the Hong Kong Special Administrative Region shall be four years, except the first term which shall be two years.

Article 70
If the Legislative Council of the Hong Kong Special Administrative Region is dissolved by the Chief Executive in accordance with the provisions of this Law, it must, within three months, be reconstituted by election in accordance with Article 68 of this Law.

Article 71
The President of the Legislative Council of the Hong Kong Special Administrative Region shall be elected by and from among the members of the Legislative Council.

The President of the Legislative Council of the Hong Kong Special Administrative Region shall be a Chinese citizen of not less than 40 years of age, who is a permanent resident of the Region with no right of abode in any foreign country and has ordinarily resided in Hong Kong for a continuous period of not less than 20 years.

Article 72

The President of the Legislative Council of the Hong Kong Special Administrative Region shall exercise the following powers and functions:

(1) To preside over meetings;
(2) To decide on the agenda, giving priority to government bills for inclusion in the agenda;
(3) To decide on the time of meetings;
(4) To call special sessions during the recess;
(5) To call emergency sessions on the request of the Chief Executive; and
(6) To exercise other powers and functions as prescribed in the rules of procedure of the Legislative Council.

Article 73

The Legislative Council of the Hong Kong Special Administrative Region shall exercise the following powers and functions:

(1) To enact, amend or repeal laws in accordance with the provisions of this Law and legal procedures;
(2) To examine and approve budgets introduced by the government;
(3) To approve taxation and public expenditure;
(4) To receive and debate the policy addresses of the Chief Executive;
(5) To raise questions on the work of the government;
(6) To debate any issue concerning public interests;
(7) To endorse the appointment and removal of the judges of the Court of Final Appeal and the Chief Judge of the High Court;
(8) To receive and handle complaints from Hong Kong residents;
(9) If a motion initiated jointly by one-fourth of all the members of the Legislative Council charges the Chief Executive with serious breach of law or dereliction of duty and if he or she refuses to resign, the Council may, after passing a motion for investigation, give a mandate to the Chief Justice of the Court of Final Appeal to form and chair an independent investigation committee. The committee shall be responsible for carrying out the investigation and reporting its findings to the Council. If the committee considers the evidence sufficient to substantiate such charges, the Council may pass a motion of impeachment by a two-thirds majority of all its members and report it to the Central People's Government for decision; and
(10) To summon, as required when exercising the above-mentioned powers and functions, persons concerned to testify or give evidence.

Article 74

Members of the Legislative Council of the Hong Kong Special Administrative Region may introduce bills in accordance with the provisions of this Law and legal procedures. Bills which do not relate to public expenditure or political structure or the operation of the government may be introduced individually or jointly by members of the Council. The written consent of the Chief Executive shall be required before bills relating to government policies are introduced.

Article 75
The quorum for the meeting of the Legislative Council of the Hong Kong Special Administrative Region shall be not less than one half of all its members.

The rules of procedure of the Legislative Council shall be made by the Council on its own, provided that they do not contravene this Law.

Article 76
A bill passed by the Legislative Council of the Hong Kong Special Administrative Region may take effect only after it is signed and promulgated by the Chief Executive.

Article 77
Members of the Legislative Council of the Hong Kong Special Administrative Region shall be immune from legal action in respect of their statements at meetings of the Council.

Article 78
Members of the Legislative Council of the Hong Kong Special Administrative Region shall not be subjected to arrest when attending or on their way to a meeting of the Council.

Article 79
The President of the Legislative Council of the Hong Kong Special Administrative Region shall declare that a member of the Council is no longer qualified for the office under any of the following circumstances:

(1) When he or she loses the ability to discharge his or her duties as a result of serious illness or other reasons;
(2) When he or she, with no valid reason, is absent from meetings for three consecutive months without the consent of the President of the Legislative Council;
(3) When he or she loses or renounces his or her status as a permanent resident of the Region;
(4) When he or she accepts a government appointment and becomes a public servant;
(5) When he or she is bankrupt or fails to comply with a court order to repay debts;
(6) When he or she is convicted and sentenced to imprisonment for one month or more for a criminal offence committed within or outside the Region and is relieved of his or her duties by a motion passed by two-thirds of the members of the Legislative Council present; and
(7) When he or she is censured for misbehaviour or breach of oath by a vote of two-thirds of the members of the Legislative Council present.

Section 4: The Judiciary

Article 80
The courts of the Hong Kong Special Administrative Region at all levels shall be the judiciary of the Region, exercising the judicial power of the Region.

Article 81

The Court of Final Appeal, the High Court, district courts, magistrates' courts and other Special courts shall be established in the Hong Kong Special Administrative Region. The High Court shall comprise the Court of Appeal and the Court of First Instance.

The judicial system previously practised in Hong Kong shall be maintained except for those changes consequent upon the establishment of the Court of Final Appeal of the Hong Kong Special Administrative Region.

Article 82

The power of final adjudication of the Hong Kong Special Administrative Region shall be vested in the Court of Final Appeal of the Region, which may as required invite judges from other common law jurisdictions to sit on the Court of Final Appeal.

Article 83

The structure, powers and functions of the courts of the Hong Kong Special Administrative Region at all levels shall be prescribed by law.

Article 84

The courts of the Hong Kong Special Administrative Region shall adjudicate cases in accordance with the laws applicable in the Region as prescribed in Article 18 of this Law and may refer to precedents of other common law jurisdictions.

Article 85

The courts of the Hong Kong Special Administrative Region shall exercise judicial power independently, free from any interference. Members of the judiciary shall be immune from legal action in the performance of their judicial functions.

Article 86

The principle of trial by jury previously practised in Hong Kong shall be maintained.

Article 87

In criminal or civil proceedings in the Hong Kong Special Administrative Region, the principles previously applied in Hong Kong and the rights previously enjoyed by parties to proceedings shall be maintained.

Anyone who is lawfully arrested shall have the right to a fair trial by the judicial organs without delay and shall be presumed innocent until convicted by the judicial organs.

Article 88

Judges of the courts of the Hong Kong Special Administrative Region shall be appointed by the Chief Executive on the recommendation of an independent commission composed of local judges, persons from the legal profession and eminent persons from other sectors.

Article 89

A judge of a court of the Hong Kong Special Administrative Region may only be removed for inability to discharge his or her duties, or for misbehaviour, by the Chief Executive on the recommendation of a tribunal appointed by the

Chief Justice of the Court of Final Appeal and consisting of not fewer than three local judges.

The Chief Justice of the Court of Final Appeal of the Hong Kong Special Administrative Region may be investigated only for inability to discharge his or her duties, or for misbehaviour, by a tribunal appointed by the Chief Executive and consisting of not fewer than five local judges and may be removed by the Chief Executive on the recommendation of the tribunal and in accordance with the procedures prescribed in this Law.

Article 90

The Chief Justice of the Court of Final Appeal and the Chief Judge of the High Court of the Hong Kong Special Administrative Region shall be Chinese citizens who are permanent residents of the Region with no right of abode in any foreign country.

In the case of the appointment or removal of judges of the Court of Final Appeal and the Chief Judge of the High Court of the Hong Kong Special Administrative Region, the Chief Executive shall, in addition to following the procedures prescribed in Articles 88 and 89 of this Law, obtain the endorsement of the Legislative Council and report such appointment or removal to the Standing Committee of the National People's Congress for the record.

Article 91

The Hong Kong Special Administrative Region shall maintain the previous system of appointment and removal of members of the judiciary other than judges.

Article 92

Judges and other members of the judiciary of the Hong Kong Special Administrative Region shall be chosen on the basis of their judicial and professional qualities and may be recruited from other common law jurisdictions.

Article 93

Judges and other members of the judiciary serving in Hong Kong before the establishment of the Hong Kong Special Administrative Region may all remain in employment and retain their seniority with pay, allowances, benefits and conditions of service no less favourable than before.

The Government of the Hong Kong Special Administrative Region shall pay to judges and other members of the judiciary who retire or leave the service in compliance with regulations, including those who have retired or left the service before the establishment of the Hong Kong Special Administrative Region, or to their dependants, all pensions, gratuities, allowances and benefits due to them on terms no less favourable than before, irrespective of their nationality or place of residence.

Article 94

On the basis of the system previously operating in Hong Kong, the Government of the Hong Kong Special Administrative Region may make provisions for local lawyers and lawyers from outside Hong Kong to work and practise in the Region.

Article 95

The Hong Kong Special Administrative Region may, through consultations and in accordance with law, maintain juridical relations with the judicial organs of other parts of the country, and they may render assistance to each other.

Article 96

With the assistance or authorization of the Central People's Government, the Government of the Hong Kong Special Administrative Region may make appropriate arrangements with foreign states for reciprocal juridical assistance.

Section 5: District Organizations

Article 97

District organizations which are not organs of political power may be established in the Hong Kong Special Administrative Region, to be consulted by the government of the Region on district administration and other affairs, or to be responsible for providing services in such fields as culture, recreation and environmental sanitation.

Article 98

The powers and functions of the district organizations and the method for their formation shall be prescribed by law.

Section 6: Public Servants

Article 99

Public servants serving in all government departments of the Hong Kong Special Administrative Region must be permanent residents of the Region, except where otherwise provided for in Article 101 of this Law regarding public servants of foreign nationalities and except for those below a certain rank as prescribed by law.

Public servants must be dedicated to their duties and be responsible to the Government of the Hong Kong Special Administrative Region.

Article 100

Public servants serving in all Hong Kong government departments, including the police department, before the establishment of the Hong Kong Special Administrative Region, may all remain in employment and retain their seniority with pay, allowances, benefits and conditions of service no less favourable than before.

Article 101

The Government of the Hong Kong Special Administrative Region may employ British and other foreign nationals previously serving in the public service in Hong Kong, or those holding permanent identity cards of the Region, to serve as public servants in government departments at all levels, but only Chinese citizens among permanent residents of the Region with no right of abode in any foreign country may fill the following posts: the Secretaries and Deputy Secretaries of Departments, Directors of Bureaux, Commissioner Against Corruption, Director of Audit, Commissioner of Police, Director of Immigration and Commissioner of Customs and Excise.

The Government of the Hong Kong Special Administrative Region may also employ British and other foreign nationals as advisers to government departments and, when required, may recruit qualified candidates from outside the Region to fill professional and technical posts in government departments. These foreign nationals shall be employed only in their individual capacities and shall be responsible to the government of the Region.

Article 102

The Government of the Hong Kong Special Administrative Region shall pay to public servants who retire or who leave the service in compliance with regulations, including those who have retired or who have left the service in compliance with regulations before the establishment of the Hong Kong Special Administrative Region, or to their dependants, all pensions, gratuities, allowances and benefits due to them on terms no less favourable than before, irrespective of their nationality or place of residence.

Article 103

The appointment and promotion of public servants shall be on the basis of their qualifications, experience and ability. Hong Kong's previous system of recruitment, employment, assessment, discipline, training and management for the public service, including special bodies for their appointment, pay and conditions of service, shall be maintained, except for any provisions for privileged treatment of foreign nationals.

Article 104

When assuming office, the Chief Executive, principal officials, members of the Executive Council and of the Legislative Council, judges of the courts at all levels and other members of the judiciary in the Hong Kong Special Administrative Region must, in accordance with law, swear to uphold the Basic Law of the Hong Kong Special Administrative Region of the People's Republic of China and swear allegiance to the Hong Kong Special Administrative Region of the People's Republic of China.

CHAPTER V: ECONOMY

Section 1: Public Finance, Monetary Affairs, Trade, Industry and Commerce

Article 105

The Hong Kong Special Administrative Region shall, in accordance with law, protect the right of individuals and legal persons to the acquisition, use, disposal and inheritance of property and their right to compensation for lawful deprivation of their property.

Such compensation shall correspond to the real value of the property concerned at the time and shall be freely convertible and paid without undue delay.

The ownership of enterprises and the investments from outside the Region shall be protected by law.

Article 106

The Hong Kong Special Administrative Region shall have independent finances.

The Hong Kong Special Administrative Region shall use its financial revenues exclusively for its own purposes, and they shall not be handed over to the Central People's Government.

The Central People's Government shall not levy taxes in the Hong Kong Special Administrative Region.

Article 107
The Hong Kong Special Administrative Region shall follow the principle of keeping expenditure within the limits of revenues in drawing up its budget, and strive to achieve a fiscal balance, avoid deficits and keep the budget commensurate with the growth rate of its gross domestic product.

Article 108
The Hong Kong Special Administrative Region shall practise an independent taxation system.

The Hong Kong Special Administrative Region shall, taking the low tax policy previously pursued in Hong Kong as reference, enact laws on its own concerning types of taxes, tax rates, tax reductions, allowances and exemptions, and other matters of taxation.

Article 109
The Government of the Hong Kong Special Administrative Region shall provide an appropriate economic and legal environment for the maintenance of the status of Hong Kong as an international financial centre.

Article 110
The monetary and financial systems of the Hong Kong Special Administrative Region shall be prescribed by law.

The Government of the Hong Kong Special Administrative Region shall, on its own, formulate monetary and financial policies, safeguard the free operation of financial business and financial markets, and regulate and supervise them in accordance with law.

Article 111
The Hong Kong dollar, as the legal tender in the Hong Kong Special Administrative Region, shall continue to circulate.

The authority to issue Hong Kong currency shall be vested in the Government of the Hong Kong Special Administrative Region. The issue of Hong Kong currency must be backed by a 100 per cent reserve fund. The system regarding the issue of Hong Kong currency and the reserve fund system shall be prescribed by law.

The Government of the Hong Kong Special Administrative Region may authorize designated banks to issue or continue to issue Hong Kong currency under statutory authority, after satisfying itself that any issue of currency will be soundly based and that the arrangements for such issue are consistent with the object of maintaining the stability of the currency.

Article 112
No foreign exchange control policies shall be applied in the Hong Kong Special Administrative Region. The Hong Kong dollar shall be freely convertible. Markets for foreign exchange, gold, securities, futures and the like shall continue.

The Government of the Hong Kong Special Administrative Region shall safeguard the free flow of capital within, into and out of the Region.

Article 113
The Exchange Fund of the Hong Kong Special Administrative Region shall be managed and controlled by the government of the Region, primarily for regulating the exchange value of the Hong Kong dollar.

Article 114
The Hong Kong Special Administrative Region shall maintain the status of a free port and shall not impose any tariff unless otherwise prescribed by law.

Article 115
The Hong Kong Special Administrative Region shall pursue the policy of free trade and safeguard the free movement of goods, intangible assets and capital.

Article 116
The Hong Kong Special Administrative Region shall be a separate customs territory.

The Hong Kong Special Administrative Region may, using the name "Hong Kong, China", participate in relevant international organizations and international trade agreements (including preferential trade arrangements), such as the General Agreement on Tariffs and Trade and arrangements regarding international trade in textiles.

Export quotas, tariff preferences and other similar arrangements, which are obtained or made by the Hong Kong Special Administrative Region or which were obtained or made and remain valid, shall be enjoyed exclusively by the Region.

Article 117
The Hong Kong Special Administrative Region may issue its own certificates of origin for products in accordance with prevailing rules of origin.

Article 118
The Government of the Hong Kong Special Administrative Region shall provide an economic and legal environment for encouraging investments, technological progress and the development of new industries.

Article 119
The Government of the Hong Kong Special Administrative Region shall formulate appropriate policies to promote and co-ordinate the development of various trades such as manufacturing, commerce, tourism, real estate, transport, public utilities, services, agriculture and fisheries, and pay regard to the protection of the environment.

Section 2: Land Leases

Article 120
All leases of land granted, decided upon or renewed before the establishment of the Hong Kong Special Administrative Region which extend beyond 30 June 1997, and all rights in relation to such leases, shall continue to be recognized and protected under the law of the Region.

Article 121
As regards all leases of land granted or renewed where the original leases contain no right of renewal, during the period from 27 May 1985 to 30 June 1997, which extend beyond 30 June 1997 and expire not later than 30 June 2047, the lessee is not required to pay an additional premium as from 1 July 1997, but an annual

rent equivalent to 3 per cent of the rateable value of the property at that date, adjusted in step with any changes in the rateable value thereafter, shall be charged.

Article 122
In the case of old schedule lots, village lots, small houses and similar rural holdings, where the property was on 30 June 1984 held by, or, in the case of small houses granted after that date, where the property is granted to, a lessee descended through the male line from a person who was in 1898 a resident of an established village in Hong Kong, the previous rent shall remain unchanged so long as the property is held by that lessee or by one of his lawful successors in the male line.

Article 123
Where leases of land without a right of renewal expire after the establishment of the Hong Kong Special Administrative Region, they shall be dealt with in accordance with laws and policies formulated by the Region on its own.

Section 3: Shipping

Article 124
The Hong Kong Special Administrative Region shall maintain Hong Kong's previous systems of shipping management and shipping regulation, including the system for regulating conditions of seamen.

The Government of the Hong Kong Special Administrative Region shall, on its own, define its specific functions and responsibilities in respect of shipping.

Article 125
The Hong Kong Special Administrative Region shall be authorized by the Central People's Government to continue to maintain a shipping register and issue related certificates under its legislation, using the name "Hong Kong, China".

Article 126
With the exception of foreign warships, access for which requires the special permission of the Central People's Government, ships shall enjoy access to the ports of the Hong Kong Special Administrative Region in accordance with the laws of the Region.

Article 127
Private shipping businesses and shipping-related businesses and private container terminals in the Hong Kong Special Administrative Region may continue to operate freely.

Section 4: Civil Aviation

Article 128
The Government of the Hong Kong Special Administrative Region shall provide conditions and take measures for the maintenance of the status of Hong Kong as a centre of international and regional aviation.

Article 129

The Hong Kong Special Administrative Region shall continue the previous system of civil aviation management in Hong Kong and keep its own aircraft register in accordance with provisions laid down by the Central People's Government concerning nationality marks and registration marks of aircraft.

Access of foreign state aircraft to the Hong Kong Special Administrative Region shall require the special permission of the Central People's Government.

Article 130

The Hong Kong Special Administrative Region shall be responsible on its own for matters of routine business and technical management of civil aviation, including the management of airports, the provision of air traffic services within the flight information region of the Hong Kong Special Administrative Region, and the discharge of other responsibilities allocated to it under the regional air navigation procedures of the International Civil Aviation Organization.

Article 131

The Central People's Government shall, in consultation with the Government of the Hong Kong Special Administrative Region, make arrangements providing air services between the Region and other parts of the People's Republic of China for airlines incorporated in the Hong Kong Special Administrative Region and having their principal place of business in Hong Kong and other airlines of the People's Republic of China.

Article 132

All air service agreements providing air services between other parts of the People's Republic of China and other states and regions with stops at the Hong Kong Special Administrative Region and air services between the Hong Kong Special Administrative Region and other states and regions with stops at other parts of the People's Republic of China shall be concluded by the Central People's Government.

In concluding the air service agreements referred to in the first paragraph of this Article, the Central People's Government shall take account of the special conditions and economic interests of the Hong Kong Special Administrative Region and consult the government of the Region.

Representatives of the Government of the Hong Kong Special Administrative Region may, as members of the delegations of the Government of the People's Republic of China, participate in air service consultations conducted by the Central People's Government with foreign governments concerning arrangements for such services referred to in the first paragraph of this Article.

Article 133

Acting under specific authorizations from the Central People's Government, the Government of the Hong Kong Special Administrative Region may:

(1) renew or amend air service agreements and arrangements previously in force;

(2) negotiate and conclude new air service agreements providing routes for airlines incorporated in the Hong Kong Special Administrative Region and having their principal place of business in Hong Kong and providing rights for over-flights and technical stops; and

(3) negotiate and conclude provisional arrangements with foreign states or regions with which no air service agreements have been concluded.

All scheduled air services to, from or through Hong Kong, which do not operate to, from or through the mainland of China shall be regulated by the air service agreements or provisional arrangements referred to in this Article.

Article 134
The Central People's Government shall give the Government of the Hong Kong Special Administrative Region the authority to:

(1) negotiate and conclude with other authorities all arrangements concerning the implementation of the air service agreements and provisional arrangements referred to in Article 133 of this Law;
(2) issue licences to airlines incorporated in the Hong Kong Special Administrative Region and having their principal place of business in Hong Kong;
(3) designate such airlines under the air service agreements and provisional arrangements referred to in Article 133 of this Law; and
(4) issue permits to foreign airlines for services other than those to, from or through the mainland of China.

Article 135
Airlines incorporated and having their principal place of business in Hong Kong and businesses related to civil aviation functioning there prior to the establishment of the Hong Kong Special Administrative Region may continue to operate.

CHAPTER VI: EDUCATION, SCIENCE, CULTURE, SPORTS, RELIGION, LABOUR AND SOCIAL SERVICES

Article 136
On the basis of the previous educational system, the Government of the Hong Kong Special Administrative Region shall, on its own, formulate policies on the development and improvement of education, including policies regarding the educational system and its administration, the language of instruction, the allocation of funds, the examination system, the system of academic awards and the recognition of educational qualifications.

Community organizations and individuals may, in accordance with law, run educational undertakings of various kinds in the Hong Kong Special Administrative Region.

Article 137
Educational institutions of all kinds may retain their autonomy and enjoy academic freedom. They may continue to recruit staff and use teaching materials from outside the Hong Kong Special Administrative Region. Schools run by religious organizations may continue to provide religious education, including courses in religion.

Students shall enjoy freedom of choice of educational institutions and freedom to pursue their education outside the Hong Kong Special Administrative Region.

Article 138

The Government of the Hong Kong Special Administrative Region shall, on its own, formulate policies to develop western and traditional Chinese medicine and to improve medical and health services. Community organizations and individuals may provide various medical and health services in accordance with law.

Article 139

The Government of the Hong Kong Special Administrative Region shall, on its own, formulate policies on science and technology and protect by law achievements in scientific and technological research, patents, discoveries and inventions.

The Government of the Hong Kong Special Administrative Region shall, on its own, decide on the scientific and technological standards and specifications applicable in Hong Kong.

Article 140

The Government of the Hong Kong Special Administrative Region shall, on its own, formulate policies on culture and protect by law the achievements and the lawful rights and interests of authors in their literary and artistic creation.

Article 141

The Government of the Hong Kong Special Administrative Region shall not restrict the freedom of religious belief, interfere in the internal affairs of religious organizations or restrict religious activities which do not contravene the laws of the Region.

Religious organizations shall, in accordance with law, enjoy the rights to acquire, use, dispose of and inherit property and the right to receive financial assistance. Their previous property rights and interests shall be maintained and protected.

Religious organizations may, according to their previous practice, continue to run seminaries and other schools, hospitals and welfare institutions and to provide other social services.

Religious organizations and believers in the Hong Kong Special Administrative Region may maintain and develop their relations with religious organizations and believers elsewhere.

Article 142

The Government of the Hong Kong Special Administrative Region shall, on the basis of maintaining the previous systems concerning the professions, formulate provisions on its own for assessing the qualifications for practice in the various professions.

Persons with professional qualifications or qualifications for professional practice obtained prior to the establishment of the Hong Kong Special Administrative Region may retain their previous qualifications in accordance with the relevant regulations and codes of practice.

The Government of the Hong Kong Special Administrative Region shall continue to recognize the professions and the professional organizations recognized prior to the establishment of the Region, and these organizations may, on their own, assess and confer professional qualifications.

The Government of the Hong Kong Special Administrative Region may, as required by developments in society and in consultation with the parties concerned, recognize new professions and professional organizations.

Article 143
The Government of the Hong Kong Special Administrative Region shall, on its own, formulate policies on sports. Non-governmental sports organizations may continue to exist and develop in accordance with law.

Article 144
The Government of the Hong Kong Special Administrative Region shall maintain the policy previously practised in Hong Kong in respect of subventions for non-governmental organizations in fields such as education, medicine and health, culture, art, recreation, sports, social welfare and social work. Staff members previously serving in subvented organizations in Hong Kong may remain in their employment in accordance with the previous system.

Article 145
On the basis of the previous social welfare system, the Government of the Hong Kong Special Administrative Region shall, on its own, formulate policies on the development and improvement of this system in the light of the economic conditions and social needs.

Article 146
Voluntary organizations providing social services in the Hong Kong Special Administrative Region may, on their own, decide their forms of service, provided that the law is not contravened.

Article 147
The Hong Kong Special Administrative Region shall on its own formulate laws and policies relating to labour.

Article 148
The relationship between non-governmental organizations in fields such as education, science, technology, culture, art, sports, the professions, medicine and health, labour, social welfare and social work as well as religious organizations in the Hong Kong Special Administrative Region and their counterparts on the mainland shall be based on the principles of non-subordination, non-interference and mutual respect.

Article 149
Non-governmental organizations in fields such as education, science, technology, culture, art, sports, the professions, medicine and health, labour, social welfare and social work as well as religious organizations in the Hong Kong Special Administrative Region may maintain and develop relations with their counterparts in foreign countries and regions and with relevant international organizations. They may, as required, use the name "Hong Kong, China" in the relevant activities.

CHAPTER VII: EXTERNAL AFFAIRS

Article 150
Representatives of the Government of the Hong Kong Special Administrative Region may, as members of delegations of the Government of the People's

Republic of China, participate in negotiations at the diplomatic level directly affecting the Region conducted by the Central People's Government.

Article 151

The Hong Kong Special Administrative Region may on its own, using the name "Hong Kong, China", maintain and develop relations and conclude and implement agreements with foreign states and regions and relevant international organizations in the appropriate fields, including the economic, trade, financial and monetary, shipping, communications, tourism, cultural and sports fields.

Article 152

Representatives of the Government of the Hong Kong Special Administrative Region may, as members of delegations of the People's Republic of China, participate in international organizations or conferences in appropriate fields limited to states and affecting the Region, or may attend in such other capacity as may be permitted by the Central People's Government and the international organization or conference concerned, and may express their views, using the name "Hong Kong, China".

The Hong Kong Special Administrative Region may, using the name "Hong Kong, China", participate in international organizations and conferences not limited to states.

The Central People's Government shall take the necessary steps to ensure that the Hong Kong Special Administrative Region shall continue to retain its status in an appropriate capacity in those international organizations of which the People's Republic of China is a member and in which Hong Kong participates in one capacity or another.

The Central People's Government shall, where necessary, facilitate the continued participation of the Hong Kong Special Administrative Region in an appropriate capacity in those international organizations in which Hong Kong is a participant in one capacity or another, but of which the People's Republic of China is not a member.

Article 153

The application to the Hong Kong Special Administrative Region of international agreements to which the People's Republic of China is or becomes a party shall be decided by the Central People's Government, in accordance with the circumstances and needs of the Region, and after seeking the views of the government of the Region.

International agreements to which the People's Republic of China is not a party but which are implemented in Hong Kong may continue to be implemented in the Hong Kong Special Administrative Region. The Central People's Government shall, as necessary, authorize or assist the government of the Region to make appropriate arrangements for the application to the Region of other relevant international agreements.

Article 154

The Central People's Government shall authorize the Government of the Hong Kong Special Administrative Region to issue, in accordance with law, passports of the Hong Kong Special Administrative Region of the People's Republic of China to all Chinese citizens who hold permanent identity cards of the Region, and travel documents of the Hong Kong Special Administrative Region of the

People's Republic of China to all other persons lawfully residing in the Region. The above passports and documents shall be valid for all states and regions and shall record the holder's right to return to the Region.

The Government of the Hong Kong Special Administrative Region may apply immigration controls on entry into, stay in and departure from the Region by persons from foreign states and regions.

Article 155

The Central People's Government shall assist or authorize the Government of the Hong Kong Special Administrative Region to conclude visa abolition agreements with foreign states or regions.

Article 156

The Hong Kong Special Administrative Region may, as necessary, establish official or semi-official economic and trade missions in foreign countries and shall report the establishment of such missions to the Central People's Government for the record.

Article 157

The establishment of foreign consular and other official or semi-official missions in the Hong Kong Special Administrative Region shall require the approval of the Central People's Government.

Consular and other official missions established in Hong Kong by states which have formal diplomatic relations with the People's Republic of China may be maintained.

According to the circumstances of each case, consular and other official missions established in Hong Kong by states which have no formal diplomatic relations with the People's Republic of China may be permitted either to remain or be changed to semi-official missions.

States not recognized by the People's Republic of China may only establish non-governmental institutions in the Region.

CHAPTER VIII: INTERPRETATION AND AMENDMENT OF THE BASIC LAW

Article 158

The power of interpretation of this Law shall be vested in the Standing Committee of the National People's Congress.

The Standing Committee of the National People's Congress shall authorize the courts of the Hong Kong Special Administrative Region to interpret on their own, in adjudicating cases, the provisions of this Law which are within the limits of the autonomy of the Region.

The courts of the Hong Kong Special Administrative Region may also interpret other provisions of this Law in adjudicating cases. However, if the courts of the Region, in adjudicating cases, need to interpret the provisions of this Law concerning affairs which are the responsibility of the Central People's Government, or concerning the relationship between the Central Authorities and the Region, and if such interpretation will affect the judgments on the cases, the courts of the Region shall, before making their final judgments which are not appealable, seek an interpretation of the relevant provisions from the Standing

Committee of the National People's Congress through the Court of Final Appeal of the Region. When the Standing Committee makes an interpretation of the provisions concerned, the courts of the Region, in applying those provisions, shall follow the interpretation of the Standing Committee. However, judgments previously rendered shall not be affected.

The Standing Committee of the National People's Congress shall consult its Committee for the Basic Law of the Hong Kong Special Administrative Region before giving an interpretation of this Law.

Article 159

The power of amendment of this Law shall be vested in the National People's Congress.

The power to propose bills for amendments to this Law shall be vested in the Standing Committee of the National People's Congress, the State Council and the Hong Kong Special Administrative Region. Amendment bills from the Hong Kong Special Administrative Region shall be submitted to the National People's Congress by the delegation of the Region to the National People's Congress after obtaining the consent of two-thirds of the deputies of the Region to the National People's Congress, two-thirds of all the members of the Legislative Council of the Region, and the Chief Executive of the Region.

Before a bill for amendment to this Law is put on the agenda of the National People's Congress, the Committee for the Basic Law of the Hong Kong Special Administrative Region shall study it and submit its views.

No amendment to this Law shall contravene the established basic policies of the People's Republic of China regarding Hong Kong.

CHAPTER IX: SUPPLEMENTARY PROVISIONS

Article 160

Upon the establishment of the Hong Kong Special Administrative Region, the laws previously in force in Hong Kong shall be adopted as laws of the Region except for those which the Standing Committee of the National People's Congress declares to be in contravention of this Law. If any laws are later discovered to be in contravention of this Law, they shall be amended or cease to have force in accordance with the procedure as prescribed by this Law.

Documents, certificates, contracts, and rights and obligations valid under the laws previously in force in Hong Kong shall continue to be valid and be recognized and protected by the Hong Kong Special Administrative Region, provided that they do not contravene this Law.

ANNEX I: METHOD FOR THE SELECTION OF THE CHIEF EXECUTIVE OF THE HONG KONG SPECIAL ADMINISTRATIVE REGION

1. The Chief Executive shall be elected by a broadly representative Election Committee in accordance with this Law and appointed by the Central People's Government.

2. The Election Committee shall be composed of 800 members from the following sectors:

Industrial, commercial and financial sectors 200

The professions 200

Labour, social services, religious and other sectors 200

Members of the Legislative Council, representatives of district-based organizations, Hong Kong deputies to the National People's Congress, and representatives of Hong Kong members of the National Committee of the Chinese People's Political Consultative Conference 200

The term of office of the Election Committee shall be five years.

3. The delimitation of the various sectors, the organizations in each sector eligible to return Election Committee members and the number of such members returned by each of these organizations shall be prescribed by an electoral law enacted by the Hong Kong Special Administrative Region in accordance with the principles of democracy and openness.

Corporate bodies in various sectors shall, on their own, elect members to the Election Committee, in accordance with the number of seats allocated and the election method as prescribed by the electoral law.

Members of the Election Committee shall vote in their individual capacities.

4. Candidates for the office of Chief Executive may be nominated jointly by not less than 100 members of the Election Committee. Each member may nominate only one candidate.

5. The Election Committee shall, on the basis of the list of nominees, elect the Chief Executive designate by secret ballot on a one-person-one-vote basis. The specific election method shall be prescribed by the electoral law.

6. The first Chief Executive shall be selected in accordance with the "Decision of the National People's Congress of the People's Republic of China on the Method for the Formation of the First Government and the First Legislative Council of the Hong Kong Special Administrative Region".

7. If there is a need to amend the method for selecting the Chief Executives for the terms sub-sequent to the year 2007, such amendments must be made with the endorsement of a two-thirds majority of all the members of the Legislative Council and the consent of the Chief Executive, and they shall be reported to the Standing Committee of the National People's Congress for approval.

ANNEX II: METHOD FOR THE FORMATION OF THE LEGISLATIVE COUNCIL OF THE HONG KONG SPECIAL ADMINISTRATIVE REGION AND ITS VOTING PROCEDURES

I. Method for the formation of the Legislative Council

1. The Legislative Council of the Hong Kong Special Administrative Region shall be composed of 60 members in each term. In the first term, the Legislative Council shall be formed in accordance with the "Decision of the National People's Congress of the People's Republic of China on the Method for the Formation of the First Government and the First Legislative Council of the Hong Kong Special Administrative Region". The composition of the Legislative Council in the second and third terms shall be as follows:

Second term

Members returned by functional constituencies 30
Members returned by the Election Committee 6
Members returned by geographical constituencies through direct elections 24

Third term

Members returned by functional constituencies 30
Members returned by geographical constituencies through direct elections 30

2. Except in the case of the first Legislative Council, the above-mentioned Election Committee refers to the one provided for in Annex I of this Law. The division of geographical constituencies and the voting method for direct elections therein; the delimitation of functional sectors and corporate bodies, their seat allocation and election methods; and the method for electing members of the Legislative Council by the Election Committee shall be specified by an electoral law introduced by the Government of the Hong Kong Special Administrative Region and passed by the Legislative Council.

II. Procedures for voting on bills and motions in the Legislative Council

Unless otherwise provided for in this Law, the Legislative Council shall adopt the following procedures for voting on bills and motions:

The passage of bills introduced by the government shall require at least a simple majority vote of the members of the Legislative Council present.

The passage of motions, bills or amendments to government bills introduced by individual members of the Legislative Council shall require a simple majority vote of each of the two groups of members present: members returned by functional constituencies and those returned by geographical constituencies through direct elections and by the Election Committee.

III. Method for the formation of the Legislative Council and its voting procedures subsequent to the year 2007

With regard to the method for forming the Legislative Council of the Hong Kong Special Administrative Region and its procedures for voting on bills and motions after 2007, if there is a need to amend the provisions of this Annex, such amendments must be made with the endorsement of a two-thirds majority of all the members of the Council and the consent of the Chief Executive, and they shall be reported to the Standing Committee of the National People's Congress for the record.

ANNEX III: NATIONAL LAWS TO BE APPLIED IN THE HONG KONG SPECIAL ADMINISTRATIVE REGION

The following national laws shall be applied locally with effect from 1 July 1997 by way of promulgation or legislation by the Hong Kong Special Administrative Region:

1. Resolution on the Capital, Calendar, National Anthem and National Flag of the People's Republic of China
2. Resolution on the National Day of the People's Republic of China
3. Order on the National Emblem of the People's Republic of China Proclaimed by the Central People's Government
   Attached: Design of the national emblem, notes of explanation and instructions for use
4. Declaration of the Government of the People's Republic of China on the Territorial Sea
5. Nationality Law of the People's Republic of China
6. Regulations of the People's Republic of China Concerning Diplomatic Privileges and Immunities

The Design of the Regional Flag of the Hong Kong Special Administrative Region

The Design of the Regional Emblem of the Hong Kong Special Administrative Region

DECISION OF THE NATIONAL PEOPLE'S CONGRESS ON THE BASIC LAW OF THE HONG KONG SPECIAL ADMINISTRATIVE REGION OF THE PEOPLE'S REPUBLIC OF CHINA

Adopted by the Seventh National People's Congress at its Third Session on 4 April 1990

The Seventh National People's Congress at its Third Session adopts the Basic Law of the Hong Kong Special Administrative Region of the People's Republic of China, including Annex I, "Method for the Selection of the Chief Executive of the Hong Kong Special Administrative Region", Annex II, "Method for the Formation of the Legislative Council of the Hong Kong Special Administrative Region and Its Voting Procedures", Annex III, "National Laws to be Applied in the Hong Kong Special Administrative Region", and the designs of the regional flag and regional emblem of the Hong Kong Special Administrative Region. Article 31 of the Constitution of the People's Republic of China provides: "The state may establish special administrative regions when necessary. The systems to be instituted in special administrative regions shall be prescribed by law enacted by the National People's Congress in the light of the specific conditions." The Basic Law of the Hong Kong Special Administrative Region is constitutional as it is enacted in accordance with the Constitution of the People's Republic of China and in the light of the specific conditions of Hong Kong. The systems, policies and laws to be instituted after the establishment of the Hong Kong Special Administrative Region shall be based on the Basic Law of the Hong Kong Special Administrative Region.

The Basic Law of the Hong Kong Special Administrative Region of the People's Republic of China shall be put into effect as of 1 July 1997.

DECISION OF THE NATIONAL PEOPLE'S CONGRESS ON THE ESTABLISHMENT OF THE HONG KONG SPECIAL ADMINISTRATIVE REGION

Adopted by the Seventh National People's Congress at its Third Session on 4 April 1990

In accordance with the provisions of Article 31 and sub-paragraph 13 of Article 62 of the Constitution of the People's Republic of China, the Seventh National People's Congress decides at its Third Session:

1. that the Hong Kong Special Administrative Region is to be established as of 1 July 1997; and
2. that the area of the Hong Kong Special Administrative Region covers the Hong Kong Island, the Kowloon Peninsula, and the islands and adjacent waters under its jurisdiction. The map of the administrative division of the Hong Kong Special Administrative Region will be published by the State Council separately.

DECISION OF THE NATIONAL PEOPLE'S CONGRESS ON THE METHOD FOR THE FORMATION OF THE FIRST GOVERNMENT AND THE FIRST LEGISLATIVE COUNCIL OF THE HONG KONG SPECIAL ADMINISTRATIVE REGION

Adopted by the Seventh National People's Congress at its Third Session on 4 April 1990

1. The first Government and the first Legislative Council of the Hong Kong Special Administrative Region shall be formed in accordance with the principles of state sovereignty and smooth transition.

2. Within the year 1996, the National People's Congress shall establish a Preparatory Committee for the Hong Kong Special Administrative Region, which shall be responsible for preparing the establishment of the Region and shall prescribe the specific method for forming the first Government and the first Legislative Council in accordance with this Decision. The Preparatory Committee shall be composed of mainland members and of Hong Kong members who shall constitute not less than 50 per cent of its membership. Its chairman and members shall be appointed by the Standing Committee of the National People's Congress.

3. The Preparatory Committee for the Hong Kong Special Administrative Region shall be responsible for preparing the establishment of the Selection Committee for the First Government of the Hong Kong Special Administrative Region (the "Selection Committee").

The Selection Committee shall be composed entirely of permanent residents of Hong Kong and must be broadly representative. It shall include Hong Kong deputies to the National People's Congress, representatives of Hong Kong members of the National Committee of the Chinese People's Political Consultative Conference, persons with practical experience who have served in Hong Kong's executive, legislative and advisory organs prior to the establishment of the Hong Kong Special Administrative Region, and persons representative of various strata and sectors of society.

The Selection Committee shall be composed of 400 members in the following proportions:

Industrial, commercial and financial sectors 25 per cent
The professions 25 per cent
Labour, grass-roots, religious and other sectors 25 per cent
Former political figures, Hong Kong deputies to the National People's Congress, and representatives of Hong Kong members of the National

Committee of the Chinese People's Political Consultative Conference 25 per cent

4. The Selection Committee shall recommend the candidate for the first Chief Executive through local consultations or through nomination and election after consultations, and report the recommended candidate to the Central People's Government for appointment. The term of office of the first Chief Executive shall be the same as the regular term.

5. The Chief Executive of the Hong Kong Special Administrative Region shall be responsible for preparing the formation of the first Government of the Region in accordance with this Law.

6. The first Legislative Council of the Hong Kong Special Administrative Region shall be composed of 60 members, with 20 members returned by geographical constituencies through direct elections, 10 members returned by an election committee, and 30 members returned by functional constituencies. If the composition of the last Hong Kong Legislative Council before the establishment of the Hong Kong Special Administrative Region is in conformity with the relevant provisions of this Decision and the Basic Law of the Hong Kong Special Administrative Region, those of its members who uphold the Basic Law of the Hong Kong Special Administrative Region of the People's Republic of China and pledge allegiance to the Hong Kong Special Administrative Region of the People's Republic of China, and who meet the requirements set forth in the Basic Law of the Region may, upon confirmation by the Preparatory Committee, become members of the first Legislative Council of the Region.

The term of office of members of the first Legislative Council of the Hong Kong Special Administrative Region shall be two years.

DECISION OF THE NATIONAL PEOPLE'S CONGRESS APPROVING THE PROPOSAL BY THE DRAFTING COMMITTEE FOR THE BASIC LAW OF THE HONG KONG SPECIAL ADMINISTRATIVE REGION ON THE ESTABLISHMENT OF THE COMMITTEE FOR THE BASIC LAW OF THE HONG KONG SPECIAL ADMINISTRATIVE REGION UNDER THE STANDING COMMITTEE OF THE NATIONAL PEOPLE'S CONGRESS

Adopted by the Seventh National People's Congress at its Third Session on 4 April 1990

The Seventh National People's Congress decides at its Third Session:

1. to approve the proposal by the Drafting Committee for the Basic Law of the Hong Kong Special Administrative Region on the establishment of the Committee for the Basic Law of the Hong Kong Special Administrative Region under the Standing Committee for the National People's Congress; and
2. to establish the Committee for the Basic Law of the Hong Kong Special Administrative Region under the Standing Committee of the National People's Congress when the Basic Law of the Hong Kong Special Administrative Region of the People's Republic of China is put into effect.

Appendix:
PROPOSAL BY THE DRAFTING COMMITTEE FOR THE BASIC LAW OF THE HONG KONG SPECIAL ADMINISTRATIVE REGION ON THE ESTABLISHMENT OF THE COMMITTEE FOR THE BASIC LAW OF THE HONG KONG SPECIAL ADMINISTRATIVE REGION UNDER THE STANDING COMMITTEE OF THE NATIONAL PEOPLE'S CONGRESS

1. **Name**: The Committee for the Basic Law of the Hong Kong Special Administrative Region under the Standing Committee of the National People's Congress.
2. **Affiliation**: To be a working committee under the Standing Committee of the National People's Congress.
3. **Function**: To study questions arising from the implementation of Articles 17, 18, 158 and 159 of the Basic Law of the Hong Kong Special Administrative

Region and submit its views thereon to the Standing Committee of the National People's Congress.

4. **Composition**: Twelve members, six from the mainland and six from Hong Kong, including persons from the legal profession, appointed by the Standing Committee of the National People's Congress for a term of office of five years. Hong Kong members shall be Chinese citizens who are permanent residents of the Hong Kong Special Administrative Region with no right of abode in any foreign country and shall be nominated jointly by the Chief Executive, President of the Legislative Council and Chief Justice of the Court of Final Appeal of the Region for appointment by the Standing Committee of the National People's Congress.

APPENDIX II

A BILL

TO

Amend the Road Traffic Ordinance.

Enacted by the Governor of Hong Kong, with the advice and consent of the Legislative Council thereof.

1. Short title and commencement

(1) This Ordinance may be cited as the Road Traffic (Amendment) Ordinance 1995.

(2) Sections 2, 3, 4, 6, 7, 12, 13 and 14 come into operation on the day the Secretary for Transport appoints by notice in the Gazette.

2. Interpretation

Section 2 of the Road Traffic Ordinance (Cap. 374) is amended by adding—

"'approved breath analysing instrument' means an instrument of a type approved by the Commissioner of Police under section 39F for analysing the proportion of alcohol in a specimen of a person's breath;

'approved operator' means a member of the police force authorized by the Commissioner of Police under section 39F;

'approved screening device' means a device of a type approved by the Commissioner of Police under section 39F for indicating whether the proportion of alcohol in a person's breath is likely to exceed the prescribed limit;

'breath analysis' means an analysis of a specimen of a person's breath under section 39C;

'fail', for the purposes of sections 39B and 39C, includes refuse;

'hospital' means an institution which provides medical or surgical treatment for in-patients or out-patients;

'prescribed limit' means—

(*a*) 35 micrograms of alcohol in 100 millilitres of breath;

(*b*) 80 milligrams of alcohol in 100 millilitres of blood; or

(*c*) 107 milligrams of alcohol in 100 millilitres of urine

or such other proportion as the Secretary for Transport may notify in the Gazette under section 39G;

'screening breath test' means a preliminary test under section 39B;".

3. Application of Ordinance to trams

Section 4 (1) is amended by adding "39A, 39B, 39C, 39D, 39E," after "39,".

4. Application of Ordinance to village vehicles

Section 4A (2) is amended by adding "39A, 39B, 39C, 39D, 39E," after "39(1),".

5. Regulation of registration and licensing of vehicles

Section 6 (1) is amended—

(*a*) in paragraph (*f*)—

(i) by repealing "or allocation" and substituting ", allocation, cancellation or withdrawal";

(ii) by repealing ", not exceeding $1,000";

(*b*) in paragraph (*i*), by repealing "not exceeding $1,000,".

6. Driving a motor vehicle under the influence of drink or drugs

Section 39 is amended—

(*a*) in subsection (1) (*a*), by repealing "of $20,000" and substituting "at level 4";

(*b*) by repealing subsection (1) (*b*) and substituting—

"(*b*) on summary conviction on a first offence to a fine at level 3 and to imprisonment for 6 months and on a second or subsequent conviction or on a conviction subsequent to a conviction under section 39A, 39B or 39C to a fine at level 4 and to imprisonment for 12 months.";

(*c*) by repealing subsection (2) and substituting—

"(2) The court or magistrate convicting a person of an offence under this section shall disqualify him from driving for a period of not less than 2 years for a second or subsequent conviction or for a conviction subsequent to a conviction under section 39A, 39B or 39C unless for special reasons the court or magistrate orders that he be disqualified for a shorter period or that he not be disqualified.

(3) The court or magistrate may deal with the offence as a first offence when a period of 5 years has elapsed since the person's last conviction under this section or section 39A, 39B or 39C.

(4) A person is deemed not to have been in charge of a motor vehicle if he proves that at the material time the circumstances were such that there was no likelihood of his driving the motor vehicle so long as he remained under the influence of drink or drugs to such an extent as to be incapable of having proper control of the motor vehicle.

(5) The court or magistrate may, in determining whether there was such a likelihood as is mentioned in subsection (4), disregard any injury to him and any damage to the vehicle.".

7. Sections added

The following are added—

"39A. Driving, attempting to drive or being in charge of a motor vehicle with alcohol concentration above prescribed limit

(1) A person who drives or attempts to drive a motor vehicle, or is in charge of a motor vehicle, on any road with the proportion of alcohol in his breath, blood or urine exceeding the prescribed limit, commits and offence and is liable—

(*a*) on conviction on indictment to a fine at level 4 and to imprisonment for 3 years; and

(*b*) on summary conviction on a first offence to a fine at level 3 and to imprisonment for 6 months and on a second or subsequent conviction or on a conviction subsequent to a conviction under section 39, 39B or 39C to a fine at level 4 and to imprisonment for 12 months.

(2) The court or magistrate convicting a person of an offence under this section shall disqualify him from driving for a period of not less than 2 years for a second or subsequent conviction or for a conviction subsequent to a conviction under section 39, 39B or 39C unless for special reasons the court or magistrate orders that he be disqualified for a shorter period or that he not be disqualified.

(3) The court or magistrate may deal with the offence as a first offence when a period of 5 years has elapsed since the person's last conviction under this section or section 39, 39B or 39C.

(4) A person is deemed not to have been in charge of a motor vehicle if he proves that at the material time the circumstances were such that there was no likelihood of his driving the motor vehicle while the proportion of alcohol in his breath, blood or urine remained likely to exceed the prescribed limit.

(5) The court or magistrate may, in determining whether there was such a likelihood as is mentioned in subsection (4), disregard any injury to him and any damage to the vehicle.

39B. Screening breath tests

(1) A police officer in uniform may require a person to provide a specimen of breath for a screening breath test where the police officer has reasonable cause to suspect—

(*a*) that the person driving or attempting to drive or in charge of a motor vehicle on a road has alcohol in his body or has committed a traffic offence while the vehicle was in motion; or

(*b*) that the person has been driving or attempting to drive or been in charge of a motor vehicle on a road with alcohol in his body and that the person still has alcohol in his body; or

(*c*) that the person has been driving or attempting to drive or been in charge of a motor vehicle on a road and has committed a traffic offence while the vehicle was in motion.

(2) If an accident occurs owing to the presence of a motor vehicle on any road, a police officer in uniform may require a person, whom the police officer has reasonable cause to believe was driving or attempting to drive or in charge of the vehicle at the time of the accident, to provide a specimen of breath for a screening breath test.

(3) A police officer in uniform may require a person to provide a specimen at or near the place where the requirement is made under subsection (1).

(4) A police officer in uniform may require a person to provide a specimen under subsection (2) either at or near the place where the requirement is made or at a police station or hospital specified by the police officer.

(5) A police officer shall warn a person at the time of requiring a specimen for a screening breath test under this section that a failure to provide it may render him liable to prosection.

(6) A person who, without reasonable excuse, fails to provide a specimen of breath when required under this section commits an offence and it liable—

(*a*) on conviction on indictment to a fine at level 4 and to imprisonment for 3 years; and

(*b*) on summary conviction on a first offence to a fine at level 3 and to imprisonment for 6 months and on a second or subsequent conviction or on a conviction subsequent to a conviction under section 39, 39A or 39C to a fine at level 4 and to imprisonment for 12 months.

(7) The court or magistrate convicting a person of an offence under this section shall disqualify him from driving for a period of not less than 2 years for a second or subsequent conviction or for a conviction subsequent to a conviction under section 39, 39A or 39C unless for special reasons the court or magistrate orders that he be disqualified for a shorter period or that he not be disqualified.

(8) The court or magistrate may deal with the offence as a first offence when a period of 5 years has elapsed since the person's last conviction under this section or section 39, 39A or 39C.

(9) A police office in uniform may arrest a person without warrant if—

(*a*) as a result of a screening breath test he has reasonable cause to suspect that the proportion of alcohol in that person's breath exceeds the prescribed limit; or

(*b*) the person has failed to provide a specimen of breath for a screening breath test when required to do so under this section.

(10) A person fails to provide a specimen for a screening breath test unless the specimen—

(*a*) is sufficient to enable the test to be carried out; and

(*b*) is provided in a way to enable the objective of the test to be satisfactorily achieved.

39C. Provision of specimens for analysis

(1) A police officer may require a person whose screening breath test indicates that the proportion of alcohol in that person's breath is likely to exceed the prescribed limit or who fails to provide a specimen for the screening breath test with reasonable excuse—

(*a*) to provide 2 specimens of breath for analysis by means of an approved breath analysing instrument; or

(*b*) to provide a specimen of blood or urine for a labouratory test.

(2) The police officer shall decide that the person is to provide a specimen of blood or urine if—

(*a*) the police officer has reasonable cause to believe that for medical reasons a specimen of breath cannot be provided or should not be required; or

(*b*) at the time the requirement is made, an approved breath analysing instrument is not available at the police station or it is for any other reason not practicable to use an approved breath analysing instrument.

(3) Evidence of the proportion of alcohol in a specimen of breath, blood or urine may be given by the production of a document which purports to be either—

(*a*) a statement automatically produced by the approved breath analysing instrument by which the proportion of alcohol in a specimen of breath was measured and a certificate signed by an approved operator (which may but need not be contained in the same document as the statement) that the statement relates to a specimen provided by the accused at the date and time shown in the statement and that the approved breath analysing instrument was operated correctly and properly when the specimen of breath was being taken; or

(*b*) a certificate under section 25 of the Evidence Ordinance (Cap. 8) as to the proportion of alcohol found in a specimen of blood or urine identified in the certificate.

(4) Evidence that a specimen of blood was taken from the accused with his consent by a medical practitioner may be given by the production of a document purporting to certify that fact and purporting to be signed by a medical practitioner.

(5) Evidence that a specimen of urine was taken from the accused by a police officer or a medical practitioner may be given by the production of a document purporting to certify that fat and purporting to be signed by a police officer or a medical practitioner, as the case may be.

(6) A requirement under this section to provide a specimen of breath can only be made at a police station or at a hospital.

(7) A requirement under this section to provide a specimen of blood can only be made at a hospital.

(8) A requirement under this section to provide a specimen of urine can only be made at a police station or at a hospital and the police officer making the requirement shall decide whether the specimen of urine is to be provided at a police station or at a hospital.

(9) The police officer requiring the provision of a specimen other than a specimen of breath under this section shall decide whether a specimen is to be of blood or of urine, but if a medical practitioner is of the opinion that for medical reasons a specimen of blood cannot or should not be taken the specimen shall be a specimen of urine.

(10) If the police officer requires a person to provide a specimen of blood, the specimen of blood shall be taken by a medical practitioner specified by the police officer.

(11) Without limiting the effect of the provisions of this section, a specimen of blood shall not be taken from a person unless he consents to its being taken by a medical practitioner and it is so taken.

(12) Evidence of the proportion of alcohol in a specimen of breath, blood or urine provided by the accused shall be evidence that the proportion

of alcohol in the accused's breath, blood or urine at the time of the alleged offence was not less than that in the specimen.

(13) Where, at the time a specimen of blood or urine was provided by the accused, he asked to be provided with such a specimen, evidence of the proportion of alcohol found in the specimen is not admissible on behalf of the prosecution unless—

(*a*) the specimen in which the alcohol was found is one of 2 parts into which the specimen provided by the accused was divided at the time it was provided; and

(*b*) the other part was supplied to the accused.

(14) The person shall provide the specimen of urine within one hour of being required to provide it and after the provision of a previous specimen of urine.

(15) A person who, without reasonable excuse, fails to provide a specimen when required to do so under this section commits an offence and is liable—

(*a*) on conviction on indictment to a fine at level 4 and to imprisonment for 3 years; and

(*b*) on summary conviction on a first offence to a fine at level 3 and to imprisonment for 6 months and on a second or subsequent conviction or on a conviction subsequent to a conviction under section 39, 39A or 39B to a fine at level 4 and to imprisonment for 12 months.

(16) The court or magistrate convicting a person of an offence under this section shall disqualify him from driving for a period of not less than 2 years for a second or subsequent conviction or for a conviction subsequent to a conviction under section 39, 39A or 39B unless for special reasons the court or magistrate orders that he be disqualified for a shorter period or that he not be disqualified.

(17) The court or magistrate may deal with the offence as a first offence when a period of 5 years has elapsed since the person's last conviction under this section or section 39, 39A or 39B.

(18) A police officer shall warn a person at the time of requiring a specimen under this section that a failure to provide it may render him liable to prosecution.

(19) A person fails to provide a specimen of breath, blood or urine for analysis or laboratory test unless the specimen—

(*a*) is sufficient to enable the analysis or laboratory test to be carried out; and

(*b*) is provided in a way to enable the objective of the analysis or laboratory test to be satisfactorily achieved.

39D. Choice of specimens of breach

(1) The court or magistrate shall use the statement referred to in section 39C (3) (*a*) relating to the specimen with the lower proportion of alcohol out of the 2 specimens of breath a person provides under section 39C and shall disregard the other.

(2) If the specimen of breath with the lower proportion of alcohol contains no more than 50 micrograms of alcohol in 100 millilitres of breath, a person who has provided specimens of breath under section 39C may ask

that the specimens of breath be replaced by a specimen of blood or urine and the police officer shall decide whether it should be a specimen of blood or urine.

(3) The specimen under subsection (2) shall be a specimen of urine if a medical practitioner is of the opinion that for medical reasons a specimen of blood cannot or should not be taken.

(4) If the person then provides a specimen under subsection (2) within a reasonable time after the breath analysis, the statement referred to in section 39C (3) (*a*) of neither specimen of breath shall be used.

39E. Protection for hospital patients

(1) A persons at a hospital as a patient is not required to provide a specimen of breath for a screening breath test or breath analysis, or a specimen of blood or urine for a laboratory test unless the medical practitioner in immediate charge of his case has been notified of the proposal to make the requirement.

(2) A requirement made after the medical practitioner has been notified under subsection (1) is a requirement for the provision of a specimen at a hospital.

(3) If the medical practitioner objects on medical grounds, the requirement shall not be made.

(4) The ground on which the medical practitioner may object under subsection (3) is that the requirement or the provision of a specimen of breath for the screening breath test or breath analysis or a specimen of blood or urine for the laboratory test would be prejudicial to the proper care and treatment of the patient.

39F. Approval of instruments and operators

(1) The Commissioner of Police may by notice in the Gazette approve types of instruments as—

(*a*) an approved breath analysing instrument to analyse the proportion of alcohol in a specimen of a person's breath;

(*b*) an approved screening device for the purpose of indicating whether the proportion of alcohol in a person's breath is likely to exceed the prescribed limit.

(2) The Commissioner of Police may authorize in writing members of the police force as approved operators to carry out breath analysis using an approved breath analysing instrument.

39G. Amendment of prescribed limit

(1) The Secretary for Transport may by notice in the Gazette amend the definition of "prescribed limit" by varying the proportion of alcohol that constitutes the prescribed limit.

(2) Notice of a variation in the prescribed limit will not come into operation until after the time provided for the Legislative Council to debate the notice under section 34 of the Interpretation and General Clauses Ordinance (Cap. 1) has expired.".

8. Appointment of traffic wardens

Section 58 is amended by adding—

"(2A) For the purposes of discharging his functions under subsection (2), a traffic warden may require any person whom he reasonably suspects of having committed an offence under this Ordinance to give his name and address."

9. Provisions applicable to traffic wardens

Section 59 (6) is repealed.

10. Section substituted

Section 77H is repealed and the following substituted—

"77H. Amendment of Schedule 10

(1) The Governor may by order published in the Gazette amend Schedule 10.

(2) The Financial Secretary may by order published in the Gazette amend the fees set out in paragraph 6 of Schedule 10.".

11. Section substituted

Section 88H is repealed and the following substituted—

"88H. Amendment of Schedule 8

(1) The Governor may by order published in the Gazette amend Schedule 8.

(2) The Financial Secretary may by order published in the Gazette amend the fees set out in paragraph 6 of Schedule 8.".

12. Application of Ordinance to private roads

Section 117 is amended by adding "39A, 39B, 39C, 39D, 39E," after "39,".

13. Defence

Section 120 (1) is amended by adding "39A, 39B, 39C," after "39,".

Consequential Amendments

Road Traffic (Driving-offence Points) Ordinance

14. Schedule amended

The Schedule to the Road Traffic (Driving-offence Points) Ordinance (Cap. 375) is amended by repealing item 4 and substituting—

"4	Section 39	Driving, attempting to drive or being in charge of a motor vehicle under the influence of drink or drugs	10
4A	Section 39A	Driving, attempting to drive or being in charge of a motor vehicle with alcohol concentration above prescribed limit	10

4B	Section 39B (6)	Failing to provide a specimen of breath for screening breath test without reasonable excuse	10
4C	Section 39C (15)	Failing to provide a specimen of breath for breath analysis or a specimen of blood or urine for laboratory test without reasonable excuse	10".

Explanatory Memorandum

Clause 1 provides a short title and a commencement provision and clause 2 contains the definitions for the interpretation of the Bill.

2. Clause 5 empowers the Secretary for Transport to make regulations to cancel or withdraw special registration marks. It also removes the stipulated $1,000 ceiling on special fees to be charged for special registration marks or unassigned non-special registration marks.

3. Clause 6 revises the penalty provisions in section 39 of the Road Traffic Ordinance (Cap. 374) for the offence of driving under the influence of drink and drugs to bring them in line with the penalty scale stipulated in the Criminal Procedure (Amendment) (No. 2) Ordinance (1994) (58 of 1994). It also includes a defence provision.

4. Clause 7 adds the following sections to the Road Traffic Ordinance (Cap. 374)—

(*a*) section 39A provides that a person driving, attempting to drive or being in charge of a motor vehicle with alcohol concentration exceeding the prescribed limit commits an offence and is liable to the same penalty as provided for in sections 39, 39B and 39C;

(*b*) section 39B provides for the situations and locations under which a police officer is empowered to require a suspected drunk driver to take a screening breath test. It contains offence provisions if a person fails to provide a specimen of breath for the screening breath test. It also provides for the conditions under which a police officer may arrest a person without warrant;

(*c*) section 39C provides for the situations whereby a police officer may require a person to provide a specimen of breath for analysis or a specimen of blood or urine for a laboratory test. It deals with the evidence of the proportion of alcohol in a specimen obtained. It sets out the conditions under which the type of specimens should be required and how and where these specimens should be obtained. It also provides for the penalty provisions if a person fails to provide a specimen without reasonable excuse;

(*d*) section 39D deals with the replacement of breath specimens by specimens of blood or urine under certain circumstances;

(*e*) section 39E deals with the protection for hospital patients regarding the provisions of the specimens;

(*f*) section 39F provides for the types of instruments to be approved by the Commissioner of Police and the approved operators;

(*g*) the Secretary for Transport is empowered by section 39G to vary the prescribed limit regarding the alcohol concentration.

5. Clauses 3 and 4 extend the application of the new drunken driving legislation to both the tramway and village vehicles.

6. Clause 8 empowers a traffic warden to require a suspected traffic offender to give his name and address. Clause 9 lifts the restriction on traffic wardens to join trade unions.

7. Clauses 10 and 11 empower the Financial Secretary to vary the fees charged by car testing centres and vehicle emission testing centres.

8. Clauses 12 and 13 extend the application of drunken driving offences to the provisions relating to private roads.

9. Clause 14 adds the offences committed under sections 39A, 39B and 39C to the driving-offence points systems.

HONG KONG

ORDINANCE NO. 39 OF 1995

L.S.

I assent.

Christopher PATTEN,
Governor.
8 June 1995

An Ordinance to amend the Road Traffic Ordinance.

[9 June 1995]

Enacted by the Governor of Hong Kong, with the advice and consent of the Legislative Council thereof.

1. Short title and commencement

(1) This Ordinance may be cited as the Road Traffic (Amendment) Ordinance 1995.

(2) Sections 2, 3, 4, 6, 7, 12, 13 and 14 come into operation on the day the Secretary for Transport appoints by notice in the Gazette.

2. Interpretation

Section 2 of the Road Traffic Ordinance (Cap. 374) is amended by adding—

"'approved breath analysing instrument' means an instrument of a type approved by the Commissioner of Police under section 39F for analysing the proportion of alcohol in a specimen of a person's breath;

'approved operator' means a member of the police force authorized by the Commissioner of Police under section 39F;

'approved screening device' means a device of a type approved by the Commissioner of Police under section 39F for indicating whether the proportion of alcohol in a person's breath is likely to exceed the prescribed limit;

'breath analysis' means an analysis of a specimen of a person's breath under section 39C;

'fail', for the purposes of sections 39B and 39C, includes refuse;

'hospital' means an institution which provides medical or surgical treatment for in-patients or out-patients;

'prescribed limit' means—

(*a*) 35 micrograms of alcohol in 100 millilitres of breath;

(*b*) 80 milligrams of alcohol in 100 millilitres of blood; or

(*c*) 107 milligrams of alcohol in 100 milliliters of urine,

or such other proportion as the Secretary for Transport may notify in the Gazette under section 39G;

'screening breath test' means a preliminary test under section 39B;".

3. Application of Ordinance to trams

Section 4 (1) is amended by adding "39A, 39B, 39C, 39E," after "39,".

4. Application of Ordinance to village vehicles

Section 4A (2) is amended by adding "39A, 39B, 39C, 39D, 39E," after "39 (1),".

5. Regulation of registration and licensing of vehicles

Section 6 (1) is amended—

(*a*) in paragraph (*f*)—

(i) by repealing "or allocation" and substituting, "allocation, cancellation or withdrawal";

(ii) by repealing, "not exceeding $1,000";

(*b*) in paragraph (*i*), by repealing "not exceeding $1,000,".

6. Driving a motor vehicle under the influence of drink or drugs

Section 39 is amended—

(*a*) in subsection (1) (*a*), by repealing "of $20,000" and substituting "at level 4";

(*b*) by repealing subsection (1) (*b*) and substituting—

"(*b*) on summary conviction on a first offence to a fine at level 3 and to imprisonment for 6 months and on a second or subsequent conviction or on a conviction subsequent to a conviction under section 39A, 39B or 39C to a fine at level 4 and to imprisonment for 12 months.";

(*c*) by repealing subsection (2) and substituting—

"(2) The court or magistrate convicting a person of an offence under this section shall disqualify him from driving for a period of not less than 2 years for a second or subsequent conviction or for a conviction subsequent to a conviction under section 39A, 39B or 39C unless for special reasons the court or magistrate orders that he be disqualified for a shorter period or that he not be disqualified.

(3) The court or magistrate may deal with the offence as a first offence when a period of 5 years has elapsed since the person's last conviction under this section or section 39A, 39B or 39C.

(4) A person is deemed not to have been in charge of a motor vehicle if he proves that at the material time the circumstances were such that there was no likelihood of his driving the motor vehicle so long as he remained under the influence of drink or drugs to such an extent as to be incapable of having proper control of the motor vehicle.

(5) The court or magistrate may, in determining whether there was such a likelihood as is mentioned in subsection (4), disregard any injury to him and any damage to the vehicle.".

7. Sections added

The following are added—

"39A. Driving, attempting to drive or being in charge of a motor vehicle with alcohol concentration above prescribed limit

(1) A person who drives or attempts to drive a motor vehicle, or is in charge of a motor vehicle, on any road with the proportion of alcohol in his breath, blood or urine exceeding the prescribed limit, commits an offence and is liable—

(*a*) on conviction on indictment to a fine at level 4 and to imprisonment for 3 years; and

(*b*) on summary conviction on a first offence to a fine at level 3 and to imprisonment for 6 months and on a second or subsequent conviction or on a conviction subsequent to a conviction under section 39, 39B or 39C to a fine at level 4 and to imprisonment for 12 months.

(2) The court or magistrate convicting a person of an offence under this section shall disqualify him from driving for a period of not less than 2 years for a second or subsequent conviction or for a conviction subsequent to a conviction under section 39, 39B or 39C unless for special reasons the court or magistrate orders that he be disqualified for a shorter period or that he not be disqualified.

(3) The court or magistrate may deal with the offence as a first offence when a period of 5 years has elapsed since the person's last conviction under this section or section 39, 39B or 39C.

(4) A person is deemed not to have been in charge of a motor vehicle if he proves that at the material time the circumstances were such that there was no likelihood of his driving the motor vehicle while the proportion of alcohol in his breath, blood or urine remained likely to exceed the prescribed limit.

(5) The court or magistrate may, in determining whether there was such a likelihood as is mentioned in subsection (4), disregard any injury to him and any damage to the vehicle.

39B. Screening breath tests

(1) A police officer in uniform may require a person to provide a specimen of breath for a screening breath test where the police officer has reasonable cause to suspect—

(*a*) that the person driving or attempting to drive or in charge of a motor vehicle on a road has alcohol in his body or has committed a traffic offence while the vehicle was in motion; or

(*b*) that the person has been driving or attempting to drive or been in charge of a motor vehicle on a road with alcohol in his body and that the person still has alcohol in his body; or

(*c*) that the person has been driving or attempting to drive or been in charge of a motor vehicle on a road and has committed a traffic offence while the vehicle was in motion.

(2) If an accident occurs owing to the presence of a motor vehicle on any road, a police officer in uniform may require a person, whom the police officer has reasonable cause to suspect was driving or attempting to drive or in charge of the vehicle at the time of the accident, to provide a specimen of breath for a screening breath test.

(3) A police officer in uniform may require a person to provide a specimen at or near the place where the requirement is made under subsection (1).

(4) A police officer in uniform may require a person to provide a specimen under subsection (2) either at or near the place where the requirement is made or at a police station or hospital specified by the police officer.

(5) A police officer shall warn a person at the time of requiring a specimen for a screening breath test under this section that a failure to provide it may render him liable to prosecution.

(6) A person who, without reasonable excuse, fails to provide a specimen of breath when required under this section commits an offence and is liable—

(*a*) on conviction on indictment to a fine at level 4 and to imprisonment for 3 years; and

(*b*) on summary conviction on a first offence to a fine at level 3 and to imprisonment for 6 months and on a second or subsequent conviction or on a conviction subsequent to a conviction under section 39, 39A or 39C to a fine at level 4 and to imprisonment for 12 months.

(7) The court or magistrate convicting a person of an offence under this section shall disqualify him from driving for a period of not less than 2 years for a second or subsequent conviction or for a conviction subsequent to a conviction under section 39, 39A or 39C unless for special reasons the court or magistrate orders that he be disqualified for a shorter period or that he not be disqualified.

(8) The court or magistrate may deal with the offence as a first offence when a period of 5 years has elapsed since the person's last conviction under this section or section 39, 39A or 39C.

(9) A police officer in uniform may arrest a person without warrant if—

(*a*) as a result of a screening breath test he has reasonable cause to suspect that the proportion of alcohol in that person's breath exceeds the prescribed limit; or

(*b*) the person has failed to provide a specimen of breath for a screening breath test when required to do so under this section.

(10) A person fails to provide a specimen for a screening breath test unless the specimen—

(*a*) is sufficient to enable the test to be carried out; and

(*b*) is provided in a way to enable the objective of the test to be satisfactorily achieved.

39C. Provision of specimens for analysis

(1) A police officer may require a person whose screening breath test indicates that the proportion of alcohol in that person's breath is likely to exceed the prescribed limit or who fails to provide a specimen for the screening breath test with reasonable excuse—

(*a*) to provide 2 specimens of breath for analysis by means of an approved breath analysing instrument; or

(*b*) to provide a specimen of blood or urine for a laboratory test.

(2) The police officer shall decide that the person is to provide a specimen of blood or urine if—

(*a*) the police officer has reasonable cause to believe that for medical reasons a specimen of breath cannot be provided or should not be required; or

(*b*) at the time the requirement is made, an approved breath analysing instrument is not available at the police station or the hospital where the requirement is made or it is for any other reason not practicable to use an approved breath analysing instrument.

(3) Evidence of the proportion of alcohol in a specimen of breath, blood or urine may be given by the production of a document which purports to be either—

(*a*) a statement automatically produced by the approved breath analysing instrument by which the proportion of alcohol in a specimen of breath was measured and a certificate signed by an approved operator (which may but need not be contained in the same document as the statement) certifying that the statement relates to a specimen provided by the accused at the date and time shown in the statement and that the approved breath analysing instrument was operated correctly and properly when the specimen of breath was being taken; or

(*b*) a certificate under section 25 of the Evidence Ordinance (Cap. 8) as to the proportion of alcohol found in a specimen of blood or urine identified in the certificate.

(4) Evidence that a specimen of blood was taken from the accused with his consent by a medical practitioner may be given by the production of a document certifying that fact and purporting to be signed by a medical practitioner.

(5) Evidence that a specimen of urine was taken from the accused by a police officer or a medical practitioner may be given by the production of a document certifying that fact and purporting to be signed by a police officer or a medical practitioner, as the case may be.

(6) A requirement under this section to provide a specimen of breath can only be made at a police station or at a hospital.

(7) A requirement under this section to provide a specimen of blood can only be made at a hospital.

(8) A requirement under this section to provide a specimen of urine can only be made at a police station or at a hospital and the police officer making the requirement shall decide whether the specimen of urine is to be provided at a police station or at a hospital.

(9) The police officer requiring the provision of a specimen other than a specimen of breath under this section shall decide whether a specimen is to be of blood or of urine, but if a medical practitioner is of the opinion that for medical reasons a specimen of blood cannot or should not be taken the specimen shall be a specimen of urine.

(10) If the police officer requires a person to provide a specimen of blood, the specimen of blood shall be taken by a medical practitioner specified by the police officer.

(11) Without limiting the effect of the provisions of this section, a specimen of blood shall not be taken from a person unless he consents to its being taken by a medical practitioner and it is so taken.

(12) Evidence of the proportion of alcohol in a specimen of breath, blood or urine provided by the accused shall be evidence that the proportion of alcohol in the accused's breath, blood or urine at the time of the alleged offence was not less than that in the specimen.

(13) Where, at the time a specimen of blood or urine was provided by the accused, he asked to be provided with such a specimen, evidence of the proportion of alcohol found in the specimen is not admissible on behalf of the prosecution unless—

(*a*) the specimen in which the alcohol was found is one of 2 parts into which the specimen provided by the accused was divided at the time it was provided; and

(*b*) the other part was supplied to the accused.

(14) The person shall provide the specimen of urine within one hour of being required to provide it and after the provision of a previous specimen of urine.

(15) A person who, without reasonable excuse, fails to provide a specimen when required to do so under this section commits an offence and is liable—

(*a*) on conviction on indictment to a fine at level 4 and to imprisonment for 3 years; and

(*b*) on summary conviction on a first offence to a fine at level 3 and to imprisonment for 6 months and on a second or subsequent conviction or on a conviction subsequent to a conviction under section 39, 39A or 39B to a fine at level 4 and to imprisonment for 12 months.

(16) The court or magistrate convicting a person of an offence under this section shall disqualify him from driving for a period of not less than 2 years for a second or subsequent conviction or for a conviction subsequent to a conviction under section 39, 39A or 39B unless for special reasons the court or magistrate orders that he be disqualified for a shorter period or that he not be disqualified.

(17) The court or magistrate may deal with the offence as a first offence when a period of 5 years has elapsed since the person's last conviction under this section or section 39, 39A or 39B.

(18) A police officer shall warn a person at the time of requiring a specimen under this section that a failure to provide it may render him liable to prosecution.

(19) A person fails to provide a specimen of breath, blood or urine for analysis or laboratory test unless the specimen—

(*a*) is sufficient to enable the analysis or laboratory test to be carried out; and

(*b*) is provided in a way to enable the objective of the analysis or laboratory test to be satisfactorily achieved.

39D. Choice of specimens of breath

(1) The court or magistrate shall use the statement referred to in section 39C (3) (*a*) relating to the specimen with the lower proportion of alcohol out of the 2 specimens of breath a person provides under section 39C and shall disregard the other.

(2) If the specimen of breath with the lower proportion of alcohol contains no more than 50 micrograms of alcohol in 100 millilitres of breath,

a person who has provided the specimens of breath under section 39C may ask that the specimens of breath be replaced by a specimen of blood or urine and the police officer shall decide whether it should be a specimen of blood or urine.

(3) The specimen under subsection (2) shall be a specimen of urine if a medical practitioner is of the opinion that for medical reasons a specimen of blood cannot or should not be taken.

(4) If the person then provides a specimen under subsection (2) within a reasonable time after the breath analysis, the statement referred to in section 39C (3) (*a*) of neither specimen of breath shall be used.

39E. Protection for hospital patients

(1) A person at a hospital as a patient shall not be required to provide a specimen of breath for a screening breath test or breath analysis, or a specimen of blood or urine for a laboratory test unless the medical practitioner in immediate charge of his case has been notified of the proposal to make the requirement.

(2) A requirement made after the medical practitioner has been notified under subsection (1) is a requirement for the provision of a specimen at a hospital.

(3) The requirement shall not be made if the medical practitioner objects on the ground specified in subsection (4) and states in writing the diagnosis justifying the objection.

(4) The ground on which the medical practitioner may object under subsection (3) is that the requirement or the provision of a specimen of breath for the screening breath test or breath analysis or a specimen of blood or urine for the laboratory test would be prejudicial to the proper care and treatment of the patient.

39F. Approval of instruments and operators

(1) The Commissioner of Police may by notice in the Gazette approve types of instruments as—

(*a*) an approved breath analysing instrument to analyse the proportion of alcohol in a specimen of a person's breath;

(*b*) an approved screening device for the purpose of indicating whether the proportion of alcohol in a person's breath is likely to exceed the prescribed limit.

(2) The Commissioner of Police may authorize in writing members of the police force as approved operators to carry out breath analysis using an approved breath analysing instrument.

39G. Amendment of prescribed limit

(1) The Secretary for Transport may by notice in the Gazette amend the definition of "prescribed limit" by varying the proportion of alcohol that constitutes the prescribed limit.

(2) Notice of a variation in the prescribed limit will not come into operation until after the time provided for the Legislative Council to debate the notice under section 34 of the Interpretation and General Clauses Ordinance (Cap. 1) has expired.".

8. Appointment of traffic wardens

Section 58 is amended by adding—

"(2A) For the purposes of discharging his functions under subsection (2), a traffic warden may require any person whom he reasonably suspects of having committed an offence under this Ordinance to give his name and address.".

9. Provisions applicable to traffic wardens

Section 59 (6) is repealed.

10. Section substituted

Section 77H is repealed and the following substituted—

"77H. Amendment of Schedule 10

(1) The Governor may by order published in the Gazette amend Schedule 10.

(2) The Financial Secretary may by order published in the Gazette amend the fees set out in paragraph 6 of Schedule 10.".

11. Section substituted

Section 88H is repealed and the following substituted—

"88H. Amendment of Schedule 8

(1) The Governor may by order published in the Gazette amend Schedule 8.

(2) The Financial Secretary may by order published in the Gazette amend the fees set out in paragraph 6 of Schedule 8.".

12. Application of Ordinance to private roads

Section 117 is amended by adding "39A, 39B, 39C, 39D, 39E," after "39,".

13. Defence

Section 120 (1) is amended by adding "39A, 39B, 39C," after "39,".

Consequential Amendments

Road Traffic (Driving-offence Points) Ordinance

14. Schedule amended

The Schedule to the Road Traffic (Driving-offence Points) Ordinance (Cap. 375) is amended by repealing item 4 and substituting—

"4	Section 39	Driving, attempting to drive or being in charge of a motor vehicle under the influence of drink or drugs	10
4A	Section 39A	Driving, attempting to drive or being in charge of a motor vehicle with	10

		alcohol concentration above prescribed limit	
4B	Section 39B (6)	Failing to provide a specimen of breath for screening breath test without reasonable excuse	10
4C	Section 39C (15)	Failing to provide a specimen of breath for breath analysis or a specimen of blood or urine for laboratory test without reasonable excuse	10".

References

Derham, D. P., Maher, F. K. H. and Waller, P. L. *An Introduction to Law* (6th ed., Law Book Co, Sydney, 1991)

Holland, J. A. and Webb, J. S. *Learning Legal Rules* (2nd ed., Blackstone Press Ltd, London 1993)

Wesley-Smith, P. *An Introduction to the Hong Kong Legal System* (2nd ed., Oxford University Press, Hong Kong, 1993)

Index